The British Army
Today and Tomorrow

The British Army
Today and Tomorrow

Colonel H. C. B. Rogers, OBE

BOOK CLUB ASSOCIATES
LONDON

Contents

TO MY WIFE
who has spent
more than half a century
married to a
Soldier

Preface

The disposition of the British Army today differs vastly from the traditional distribution of units and establishments, during peace between the major powers, from the latter part of the 19th century until the outbreak of World War II. Until the present era the regiments were quartered either in the United Kingdom in garrison towns or training areas, or else in the countries and colonies of the Empire in localities chosen for the requirements of internal security or frontier warfare. Only in these recent times has the greater part of our fighting strength been stationed on the continent of Europe to deter, in common with Allied troops and under Allied command, a threatened attack by a common and designated enemy.

This book discusses the organisation and equipment of the Army in the light of its current deployment and possible commitments. It is divided into three parts. The first provides a background by giving a brief history of each of the major arms and services concerned with operations in the field, from the time that the introduction of the magazine rifle, the machine gun, and the quick-firing field gun changed the face of warfare, until the years immediately following World War II. The second part describes the modern weapons and equipment of the Army, particularly those introduced since the formation of the North Atlantic Treaty Organisation. And the third deals with the tactical organisations and functions of units and formations in a major war.

Acknowledgements

I am most grateful to the many officers both serving and retired, and to other persons connected with the Army who have given so much of their time and have taken so much trouble to give me information and help towards the writing of this book. I would cite particularly the following. Brig H. B. C. Watkins MBE, Editor of the *British Army Review*, has given me much information about the modern British Army and, with his expert knowledge, has helped me immensely with the illustrations. To my many calls for help, he has always responded with alacrity and enthusiasm. Lt-Col D. A. Johnson of the Directorate of Public Relations (Army) arranged briefings for me on various aspects of the Army, and through his help I was able to see most of the equipment and weapons which I have described in the book. I am in debt to him too for permission to rummage through the vast collection of photographs in the archives of the DPR(A) to select the majority of the illustrations which I have portrayed. My old friend Maj-Gen Sir Arthur Smith KBE, MC, late Colonel Commandant of the Royal Corps of Transport, wrote most of Chapter 6 himself from his own extensive knowledge of the history of supply and transport. Col P. F. G. Allardyce, Deputy Director Volunteers, Territorials and Cadets, went to a lot of trouble to give me a very clear explanation of the present situation and organisation of our Reserves, both Regular and TAVR. At the Headquarters of the Army Air Corps at Middle Wallop, Maj N. D. D. Thursby gave up a lot of time to describe the organisation and functions of his Corps, backed up by films and slides. Subsequently he corrected and amended my draft of Chapter 10 and provided me with illustrations for it. Maj R. E. W. Walsh RA, at the Headquarters of the Director Royal Artillery, explained the present organisation and equipment of the Royal Artillery and gave me most of the photographs of its equipment which appear in this book. Col A. K. Dixon, Commandant of the School of Transportation Royal Corps of Transport, arranged an excellent illustrated briefing for me on modern RCT equipment and organisation. For photographs of the Royal Corps of Signals and its predecessors I am indebted to Lt-Col D. A. Dickson, Historical Officer at Regimental Headquarters Royal Signals; for those of The King's Own Royal Border Regiment, to Lt-Col J. Petty MBE, MC, Regimental Secretary, and Lt-Col R. K. May, Curator of the Regimental Museum; and for those of The King's Own Royal Regiment to Mrs Edith Tyson, Curator of the Museum of the Regiment; all of whom took great pains in selecting the type of photographs I wanted. Finally I must mention two invaluable organisations to which I am privileged to belong, the Royal United Services Institute and the London Library.

Historical Background

1

Infantry

The regimental system of the British Army is something unique amongst the armies of the world. From 1660, the year in which the Regular Army was founded, until 1743 most infantry regiments were known by the name of their colonel. In the latter year numbers were officially allotted to the regiments of the Line in order of seniority. Numbers had, however, been used unofficially for some purposes from a few years before 1743, and regiments were still popularly known by their colonels' names for many years after that date. Numbers had the great advantage, of course, of being permanent, and with the passage of the years and the increase in battle honours borne on the Colours, the numbers embroidered on these often tattered pieces of silk became treasured symbols; so treasured, indeed, that today, nearly a hundred years after their official abolition, they have been restored in some of the present titles.

In 1881 it was decided that all Line regiments should have at least two battalions, of which in peacetime one would normally be at home and the other overseas, and that numbers should be replaced by titles, generally including the name of a county, or other indication of a regiment's recruiting area. (This was not a new idea, because county names had been given to some regiments in the past as subsidiary titles to link them with a particular area for recruiting, but they had been little used.) Except for the 1st to 25th Regiments, the 60th Rifles, and the Rifle Brigade, all regiments had only one battalion in 1881, and the reorganisation was effected by amalgamating these single-battalion regiments in pairs, calling the senior the 1st Battalion and the junior the 2nd Battalion. (The 79th, or Cameron Highlanders, escaped amalgamation because no regiment was left to pair with it.) The forced union between regiments, which generally had quite different traditions, was extremely unpopular, and there was sometimes a mutual disparagement which lasted for years. The 53rd Shropshire Regiment and the 85th Light Infantry, for instance, which became the 1st and 2nd Battalions respectively of The King's Shropshire Light Infantry, still harboured some dislike of each other in the years before World War I, and the old numbers and badges were embossed on their officers mess writing paper. At a still later date, the author remembers that when his own regiment (The 4th or King's Own Regiment of Foot) arrived at Rawalpindi in 1925 to take over from the 2nd Battalion The Oxfordshire and Buckinghamshire Light Infantry (the erstwhile 52nd), he was surprised to learn that officers posted from the 1st Battalion (the old 43rd) were regarded as barely socially acceptable.

Another break with the past was the decision in 1882 that the regimental Colours should no longer be carried into action. At the battle of Laing's Nek in 1881, during the First Boer War, an officer carrying one of the colours of the 58th Foot (which became the 2nd Battalion The Northamptonshire Regiment in the same year) was mortally wounded. This was the last occasion on which a British regiment carried its Colours on active service.

A few years later, in 1888, the historic red coat of the British soldier was worn on active service for the last time, when, as recorded by Captain McCance who served with the Regiment during the campaign, the 1st Battalion The Royal Scots were so dressed throughout the operations in Zululand.[1]

As we approach the end of the century, then, we find the British infantry forsaking the red coat, in which it had fought since its foundation, and leaving at home the Colours, typifying the soul of the regiment, which had served as a rallying point on all the major battlefields from Tangier to Kandahar. The sturdy discipline of those close-ordered ranks, latterly armed with the single-shot Martini-Henry rifle, had sufficed to defeat enemies, often greatly superior in numbers, on battlefields spread across the world in every type of terrain and climate.

In 1884, however, there were two developments which were to herald a vast change in infantry tactics, though it was to be exactly thirty years before their effects were really appreciated by the majority of both British and foreign soldiers. In that year Germany converted her 1871 pattern single-shot Mauser rifle by fitting it with a magazine, and Hiram Maxim patented a single-barrel machine gun which loaded and fired itself by using the power of its own recoil, and achieved a firing rate of 600 rounds per minute, as long as the firer pressed the trigger or until its belt of ammunition needed replacement. Two years later the French Army replaced their 1874 single-shot rifle with one which for a short time led the world: the officially named Fusil d'Infanterie Modele 1886, which was commonly known as the Lebel, after the senior officer of the committee responsible for its adoption. It incorporated a magazine, but it was additionally noteworthy for its smokeless cartridge.

In 1888 Great Britain produced an even better magazine rifle, the Lee-Metford, or Rifle Magazine Mark I, which replaced the single-shot Martini-Henry. It did, however, still use black powder, and its barrel, with a seven-groove rifling, was designed by William Metford specifically to combat the fouling caused by this powder. The bolt action and the magazine were invented by James Lee, a watchmaker by trade. The Lee bolt was strongly criticised by leading British gunsmiths because it was held in position when closed by lugs at the rear end of the bolt; whereas theoretically, in order that the minimum amount of material should be under stress at the time of firing, front locking lugs should be used as on the German Mauser. However, the Lee action is the fastest bolt action ever to have been devised, and it was retained in the British Army until the advent of automatic rifles in recent years.

To enable the firer to keep his sights on the target during rapid fire and to conceal his own position, a smokeless powder was urgently needed. A committee to examine the problem was set up under Sir Frederick Abel Bt, chemist to the War Department and Ordnance Committees and an expert on explosives. A solution was found in a preparation based on the discoveries of a great Swedish engineer, Alfred Nobel. This substance was hardened into a long cord and given the name 'cordite'. From 1892 it was used in all British small arms ammunition.

Once a smokeless powder had been introduced there was no further need for the Metford barrel, and the British magazine rifle was modified at the Royal Small Arms Factory, Enfield Lock, to incorporate more efficient rifling for a high velocity rifle, with a five-groove instead of a seven-groove barrel. The new Rifle, Magazine, Lee-Enfield Mark I was introduced on 11 November (prophetic date!) 1895. Earlier in that year another mark of Lee-Metford had been issued, and both Lee-Metfords and Lee-Enfields were used in the Boer War.

On its first introduction the magazine was conceived as a reserve to be used when rapid fire was needed in an emergency, and single-shot action was still regarded as the normal. For this reason there was a cut-out on the rifle which could be slid across the magazine, cutting it off from the chamber, and the rifle was then reloaded by hand with a single round after each shot. It was probably believed that ammunition supply would present difficulties if the magazine were used freely. Because of this conception there were no means for re-charging the magazine quickly. Lee had invented a charger in 1892, by which five rounds could be loaded simultaneously, but its adoption was not considered necessary, and the magazine had to be re-charged one round at a time.[2]

The Maxim machine gun was tested by the British Army in 1887 and adopted two years later. By 1891 it had proved its effectiveness in the field. It was not the first machine gun to be used by British forces, but its predecessors were hand-operated and of limited value. The British firm of Vickers acquired most of the patents for the Maxim gun and manufactured it in the United Kingdom.[3]

On 2 September 1898 Lord Kitchener fought and won the battle of Omdurman, the last major action in which British troops were engaged before the outbreak of the Boer War in the following year. Kitchener's army consisted of two British infantry brigades, four Egyptian and Sudanese infantry brigades, two cavalry regiments, a camel corps, and six batteries of artillery. The whole force was in a fortified camp, its perimeter lined by infantry with each flank resting upon the Nile. The Khalifa's army attacked this camp and encountered first the fire of the British field artillery, and then the rifle fire of the infantry and the machine gun fire of the Maxim gun detachments. The British infantry, with their magazine rifles, opened fire at 2,000 yards and stopped the Dervishes 500 yards from the camp perimeter. The Egyptian and Sudanese troops, armed with single-shot Martini-Henrys and firing by volleys, engaged the enemy at 1,000 yards and stopped them 300 yards away. The magazine rifles had the new cordite cartridges. The subsequent advance of Kitchener's force, well drilled and trained for this type of warfare, led to the crushing defeat and dispersal of the Khalifa's army, with a loss of some 11,000 dead and 16,000 wounded, as compared with the Anglo-Egyptian casualties of 56 dead and 434 wounded.

Probably few of those present realised that they had witnessed the end of an era, but realisation came just a year later in the second week of December 1899 — the 'Black Week'; for the British Army had encountered a very different type of foe. The Boer Army was a force of mounted infantry, armed like the British with magazine rifles (Mausers), using smokeless powder, and, mounted on their tough little ponies, able to move rapidly from place to place over a country which they knew intimately. They normally dismounted to fight, and were adept at the use of ground for cover and movement. In the war against this mobile enemy, who could deliver rapid and accurate fire from concealed positions, it was soon apparent that the old rigid tactics would no longer serve. In one week the Boers defeated Buller at Colenso, Gatacre at Stormberg, and Lord Methuen at Magersfontein. Magersfontein, particularly, provided a foretaste of World War I, for photographs show the deep, well constructed, and well sited trenches, from which the Boers brought such heavy fire to bear on the British attack. Furthermore, those trenches were protected by barbed wire, and, a little time later, pliers to cut barbed wire entanglements were advertised in the British press.[4]

On 10 January 1900 Lord Roberts arrived in Cape Town as Commander-in-Chief. Within three weeks he had issued two instructions on tactics. These directed that advances were to be carried out in open order; men were to be trained in the skilful use of cover; instead of direct frontal attack, outflanking movements were to be used as far as possible; scouting was to be improved; and junior officers were to use more initiative.[5] In addition, to provide the mobility he wanted, Roberts greatly increased his strength of mounted infantry. With measures such as these, it was not long before the British infantry attained a mastery of the battlefield; and it was as a result of Roberts' teaching that they were to enter the First World War as the best trained infantry in Europe.

Mounted infantry had been formed in small numbers for previous campaigns in Africa, but it was in the Boer War that they really came into their own. In addition to units, such as the Imperial Yeomanry, sent out especially from home, fifteen battalions were formed from infantry regiments serving in South Africa. They were not intended to supplement or replace cavalry, for cavalry were trained primarily to fight mounted, whereas mounted infantry used their horses or ponies for mobility and fought dismounted. It was the same difference, in a later age, between tanks and armoured personnel carriers. It is of some interest that in the 'Evidence taken before the Royal Commission on the War in South Africa' the future Field-Marshal Earl Haig said that rather than mounted infantry he would prefer infantry 'on motors'.[6]

Maxim machine guns were issued on a scale of one to each battalion in the Boer War. The gun was carried on a special machine gun carriage, drawn by a horse or mule between shafts, and there was a fitting for 'man draught'. (The author's father once assured him that the contemporary regulations said that the machine gun carriage was to be pulled by a mule or an intelligent NCO!) The carriage was fitted to carry ammunition boxes and all the stores required for the gun, which could be fired either from its carriage or from a separate tripod mount.[7] The Boers had a few Maxims which had been supplied to them by Messrs. Vickers; War Office permission having been given on the grounds that if the Boers could not buy them from Great Britain they would get them from somewhere else.

As a result of the lessons of the Boer War, a shortened version of the Lee Enfield rifle was introduced in 1903. This was the Short Magazine Lee Enfield (SMLE), intended as a universal weapon which could replace the cavalry's carbine without lessening its efficiency as a rifle for the infantry. There were various marks, and as finally developed it was the finest bolt action rifle ever devised and familiar to countless soldiers for the following half century.

One of the few people who foretold something of the effects of the new weapons in a future war was a Polish banker named I. S. Bloch. In a conversation with the British journalist W. T. Stead he said that 'the outward and visible sign of the end of war was the introduction of the magazine rifle, and he wrote in a book that the next war would be a kind of stalemate, with everybody entrenched and the spade as indispensable to the soldier as his rifle.[8] Bloch, of course, was unduly optimistic in believing that the magazine rifle would make war impossible; but the deadliness of the new fire power was apparent when, in accordance with the French policy of the offensive, infantry were thrown into close order attack in the 'Battle of the Frontiers' in 1914 and were defeated with a massive casualty list of 300,000 men.[9]

The only infantry trained for modern war were the British. Of the 1914 BEF, Sir Basil Liddell Hart said, 'Small as to size, it enjoyed a practical and varied experience without parallel among the continental armies.'[10] He goes on to say that no battle in Britain's annals had given clearer proof of the fighting quality of the British Regular Army than 'First Ypres' in 1914. 'Such was the ability', he writes, 'of the British infantry to produce "fifteen rounds rapid" a minute that the Germans credited them with "quantities of machine guns."' He draws attention to the unique corporate sense of the British Army due to its regimental system, and ends nicely with: '"First Ypres", on the British side, was not merely a soldiers' battle but a "family battle" against outsiders.' Of this same battle, Liddell Hart quotes the statement by Sir James Edmonds in his Official History that: 'The line that stood between the British Empire and ruin was composed of tired, haggard, and unshaven men, unwashed, plastered with mud, many in little more than rags.'[11]

World War I stretched a regimental system based generally on two Regular battalions, with two Territorial battalions for home defence. The infantry battalions of the vast new armies that were raised, first from volunteers and later from conscripts, were all additional battalions of the existing regiments. The conception was good, but the unequal distribution of heavy casualties resulted all too frequently in reinforcement drafts from the United Kingdom being sent to regiments other than those whose badge they wore.

In November 1912 the Vickers machine gun, an improved version of the Maxim, had been adopted for use in the British Army and issued to the infantry on a scale of two per battalion. This excellent gun was destined to remain the standard support-fire machine gun until the middle 1960s. The power of the machine gun to dominate the battlefield was such that all the contending armies were soon equipped with considerably greater numbers. In the British Army the Machine Gun Corps was formed and armed with the Vickers gun, and a battalion of the Corps was incorporated in the establishment of each infantry division.

However, the Vickers was essentially an infantry support weapon, and a demand arose for a much more portable machine gun that could be issued to infantry platoons.

In America, before World War I, Colonel Isaac Lewis had designed a heavy or medium machine gun from ideas originated by Samuel Maclean. This was suitable for conversion to a light machine gun and as such it was adopted by the Belgian Army in 1913. Soon afterwards the British Army expressed an interest in it, and the Birmingham Small Arms Company obtained manufacturing rights.[12] After an initial issue of eight to a battalion, every platoon in due course had its Lewis gun section. It was a very popular weapon and, though prone to stoppages, these were generally easily cleared. The cocking handle could stop in one of three positions and the action to be taken on each formed part of the instruction on the gun. ('Gun stops in first position!' a sergeant instructor would call out, and a very junior subaltern at the Small Arms School, Pachmarhi, in 1925, would be expected to take rapid and appropriate action!)

Trench warfare demanded a close-support weapon which could lob projectiles into enemy trenches, and the answer was found in the very effective and simple Stokes mortar. Each infantry brigade had a battery of these. Lastly, for the frequent close range fighting of trench warfare, the Mills hand grenade was designed, and this could also, with a special attachment, be fired from a rifle. The grenade became so popular that it largely supplanted the rifle, with a consequent marked deterioration in the skilled use of that weapon.

Between the two world wars the minor campaigns of the Empire were fought by infantry equipped with the same weapons and trained in the light of the lessons of World War I. Rifle shooting, however, resumed its old importance and the annual range practice was the prime factor in the training of the individual.

But from the very limited amount that the Government was prepared to spend on defence during the major part of this period, the Army was allotted the least. It was, in the words of M. M. Postan, the 'Cinderella' Service.[13] At home the equipment scales of the infantry were deplorable. It was common on exercises, for instance, to see machine guns represented by signal flags or by DP (drill purposes only) rifles painted with coloured bands. Mechanisation began slowly in 1929, but it was 1934 before a start was made in replacing the animal transport of the infantry.[14]

In 1933, in its search for a replacement for the Lewis light machine gun, the War Office chose the Czech Zbrojowka vz26, which was brought to Great Britain by the British military attache in Prague. This was modified and manufactured by the Royal Small Arms Factory at Enfield Lock, and called the Bren, derived from the town of Brno where the original gun was made. This was an excellent light machine gun, but it was 1937 before the first batch of Brens reached battalions.[15]

Another addition to the infantry's armament was the Boys anti-tank rifle, which was capable of piercing the armour of light tanks and armoured cars.

In 1926 the Short Magazine Lee Enfield was re-designated the No 1 rifle, a title of which, however, the bulk of the Army remained in blissful ignorance. The gradual appearance from 1931 onwards of a No 4 rifle therefore caused some slight bewilderment, until it was appreciated that it was merely the SMLE slightly modified to aid mass production and with a heavier barrel to improve the accuracy of the shooting. This was the rifle of World War II and was a very popular and serviceable weapon. Not so popular, however, was a miserable little rounded prong of a bayonet; too inconspicuous to have the moral effect of the sword bayonet and of little use for the many useful, if illegitimate, purposes to which a bayonet is put. It was later replaced by a short sword bayonet.[16]

An infantry battalion in the British Expeditionary Force of 1939-1940 was armed with 50 Bren light machine guns, two 3in mortars, 12 2in mortars, and 22 Boys anti-tank rifles. There were also 10 armoured tracked carriers, each mounting a Bren gun, and commonly known in fact as Bren carriers. The Vickers guns were all in machine gun battalions, of which there were four as GHQ troops and three in each corps as corps troops. The Machine Gun Corps had not been recreated, and these were ordinary Regular and Territorial battalions which had been reorganised. Each battalion had 48 Vickers guns and 18 Bren guns.[17]

The British infantry in World War II displayed the same tenacious stubbornness in battle as it did in World War I. One instance, again taken from the early part of the war, will suffice. This was the defence of Calais in 1940 by the 30th Brigade of the 1st Armoured Division, in which the infantry units were the 2nd Battalion The King's Royal Rifle Corps, the 1st Battalion The Rifle Brigade, and the 1st Battalion Queen Victoria's Rifles, TA. Of their epic fight, the Official History writes:

'The troops who held Calais fought against overwhelming odds with a cheerful courage and unquestioning devotion to duty which match the finest traditions of the British Army . . . They gained the distinction of having fought to the end, at a high cost of life and liberty, because this was required of them. They helped to make it possible for the British Expeditionary Force to reach Dunkirk and by their disciplined courage and stout-hearted endurance they enriched the history of the British Army.'[18]

In August 1940 German divisions training for the invasion of England were provided with the following report prepared by the German IV Corps, which had been fighting against the BEF from the first contact on the River Dyle in Belgium until the evacuation from Dunkirk and the neighbouring beaches:

'The English soldier was in excellent physical condition. He bore his own wounds with stoical calm. The losses of his own troops he discussed with complete equanimity. He did not complain of hardships. In battle he was tough and dogged. His conviction that England would conquer in the end was unshakeable. The English soldier has always shown himself to be a fighter of high value. Certainly the Territorial divisions are inferior to the Regular troops in training, but where morale is concerned they are their equal.'[19]

Below: **2nd Battalion The King's Own (Royal Lancaster) Regiment en route to Spion Kop, Boer War (photo: The Rev Hill, Chaplain to the Forces, Natal Field Force).** / *Museum of The King's Own Royal Regiment (Lancaster)*

The prominent part played by tanks in World War II resulted inevitably in alterations in the equipment of the infantry. The Boys anti-tank rifle was of little use when thicker steel plate defied its employment against armoured fighting vehicles. The infantry motor battalions, of which one normally formed the infantry element of an armoured brigade, were armed at first with the 2-pounder anti-tank gun and later with the 6-pounder. At the second battle of El Alamein the 6-pounder guns of the 7th Battalion The Rifle Brigade (The London Rifle Brigade) provided the first example of infantry repelling a tank attack with its own weapons.[20]

A notable infantry anti-tank weapon produced later in the War was the spigot mortar, known as the PIAT (Projector Infantry Anti-Tank), which was very effective at ranges of from 150 to 250 yards. The projectile, a hollow charge type, was attached to a tube with a cartridge at the front end. The tube was slipped over a rod or spigot. When the mortar was fired the tube and hollow charge projectile were discharged together, the tube providing the stability to maintain direction in flight. The infantry's conventional mortars were the 2in and the 3in.[21]

Communications within the battalion were mainly by wireless; a great change from the line, heliograph, daylight signalling lamp, and flag of the First World War and for many years after it.

Before World War II most infantry regiments had one battalion in the United Kingdom and the other overseas, generally in India. The rapid contraction of the Empire after the war led to a decision to reduce all infantry regiments to one Regular battalion. Even after this measure there were still more infantry battalions than were required because of alterations in the proportions of the various arms. A large number of regiments were therefore amalgamated. This was a much more drastic amalgamation than that of 1881, because on that occasion each battalion

preserved the identity of the previous regiment. The next step in this post-Imperial organisation was to group the one-battalion regiments into administrative brigades, each composed of from three to five regiments from the same area or of a similar type; eg the Brigade of Guards and the Lancashire Brigade. The object of this grouping was to provide a wider sphere for promotion, reinforcement, etc, by cross-posting between the regiments. To make this relationship even closer, regiments in each of these brigades were allowed, if they so wished, to amalgamate to form so-called 'large regiments'; the battalions of the old regiments then became the 1st, 2nd, 3rd, etc of the new large regiments. In 1969 centralisation was taken still further by grouping brigades and large regiments into administrative divisions. These were the Guards, the Scottish, the Queen's, the King's, the Prince of Wales's, and the Light. The order of precedence (as given) followed that of the old number of the senior regiment in each of the Line divisions: ie Scottish the 1st or Royal Scots; Queen's, the 2nd or Queen's Royal Regiment; King's, the 4th or King's Own Royal Regiment; Prince of Wales's, the 11th or Devonshire Regiment; and Light, the 13th or Somerset Light Infantry. The Parachute Regiment and the Brigade of Gurkhas were excluded from these divisions.[22] These various reorganisations are complex and the amalgamations of the different regiments from the pre-1881 numbers to the present day are set out in the Appendix.

Below: **4th (Militia) Battalion The King's Own (Royal Lancaster) Regiment at Joubert's Siding, near Colesberg, 'throwing up trenches'; Boer War.** / *Museum of The King's Own Royal Regiment (Lancaster)*

Bottom: **4th (Militia) Battalion The King's Own (Royal Lancaster) Regiment striking camp at De Aar; Boer War.** / *Museum of The King's Own Royal Regiment (Lancaster)*

Above left: **The 2nd and 3rd Service Companies of the 1st Volunteer Battalion The King's Own (Royal Lancaster) Regiment crossing Sand Spruit; Boer War.** / *Museum of The King's Own Royal Regiment (Lancaster)*

Above: **'A happy home inside the trenches at Loos'. Winter 1915. Pte Carr, Pte Thompson, and Sgt Clowes.** / *Museum of The King's Own Royal Regiment (Lancaster)*

Left: **1st/5th Battalion The King's Own (Royal Lancaster) Regiment. Soldiers rejoining the Battalion at Winninzeel, Belgium, 1915.** / *Museum of The King's Own Royal Regiment (Lancaster)*

Below: **1st/5th Battalion The King's Own (Royal Lancaster) Regiment in the Zillebeke trenches, May 1915.** / *Museum of The King's Own Royal Regiment (Lancaster)*

Top: Presentation of new Colours to the 2nd Battalion The King's Own Royal Regiment (Lancaster) by Field Marshal Sir Claude Jacob; Rawalpindi 1926. (The author is second from the right in the back row, carrying the old King's Colour with its heavy wreath.) / *Museum of The King's Own Royal Regiment (Lancaster)*

Above: B Company, 1st Battalion The King's Own Royal Regiment, coming out of action over the Pideura Ridge, Christmas 1944. / *Museum of The King's Own Royal Regiment (Lancaster)*

Right: 1st Battalion The King's Own Royal Regiment, Italy 1944. Supplies being brought forward by mule under the command of Colour Sergeant Lycett. / *Museum of The King's Own Royal Regiment (Lancaster)*

2
Cavalry and Armour

Horsed cavalry and their armoured vehicle successors perform the same tactical function; that is, mounted shock action, reconnaissance, and protection. In the great days of the horse soldier, heavy cavalry, composed of big men on big horses, were intended primarily for the massed charge, whereas light cavalry, with smaller men on lighter horses, undertook the duties of outposts, advanced, flank, and rear guards, and reconnaissance. In practice, light cavalry were often employed in the main battle, and ultimately there was little difference in the use of the two categories. The advent of the magazine rifle and the machine gun, however, made the cavalry charge impracticable, except in exploiting success or in seizing an opportunity presented by surprise. But during the Boer War this had not yet been appreciated, and cavalry commanders tended to reserve thier horses for the decisive moment of the massed charge. The result was that cavalry were not available to the Commander-in-Chief to the extent they should have been. In a letter which Lord Roberts wrote to Erskine Childers, in connection with the latter's book *War and the Arme Blanche*, he said, of his operations against the Boers:

'I hoped that by turning their flanks the mounted portions of the force would have fallen upon them as they were retreating. But in this... I was invariably disappointed owing to quite small parties of Boers being able to keep off whole Brigades of Cavalry, and to the Cavalry themselves never having been taught to fight under the altered conditions of modern warfare.'[1]

Cavalry were not, on the whole, trained to fight dismounted at this period. In about 1878 the Martini-Henry single shot carbine was in general issue, but it was not received very enthusiastically, particularly by lancers who had previously been equipped with no firearms other than pistols. Indeed, it has been recorded that one regiment of lancers, when it first received carbines, loaded them on to stable barrows and wheeled them to a manure heap![2]

In 1874 the Martini-Henry carbine was replaced by the Lee-Metford carbine, which was very similar to the rifle, except for a very much shorter barrel.[3] The range of this weapon was far too short, and, as recorded in Chapter 1, the cavalry were in 1903 issued with the Short Magazine Lee-Enfield (SMLE) rifle. The lessons of the Boer War had by this time borne fruit, and dismounted action played a large part in cavalry training.

On the Western Front in World War I cavalry could only be used during mobile operations. They were of value in the early operations of 1914 and in harassing and delaying the German advances during their great spring offensive of 1918; and in the decisive battle of Amiens in August 1918 cavalry played a notable part, until machine gun fire and barbed wire frustrated all efforts to exploit victory.

Because cavalry could no longer fulfil its shock action role, on account of the vulnerability of its mount, a tracked and armoured mechanical mount was designed to replace it. This was the tank, which had its first major success at the battle of Cambrai towards the end of 1917, and then won the decisive battle of the war when a massed attack by over 400 tanks broke the German defence on 8 August 1918 — a date which General Ludendorff called 'the black day of the German Army'.

The heavy tank of World War I, though maintaining its basic shape, was developed through a number of versions to the final Mark V and Mark VI (the latter being a lengthened version to carry infantry machine gun crews forward to hold positions). Seen broadside, the tank was a rhomboid, with upturned nose and a slope down at the rear, having its tracks carried right round the body. There were two types, classified respectively as 'Male' and 'Female'. The former was armed with two 6-pounder QF Hotchkiss guns mounted one on each side of the hull in large sponsons, and four Lewis light machine guns. The latter, the function of which was to give close support to the gun tank against infantry, was armed with four Vickers machine guns, two in each sponson, and one Lewis gun. The Mark V, though slightly faster than its predecessors, had a road speed of only 4.6mph. In March 1918 the Medium Mark A tank, commonly known as the Whippet, went into action for the first time. This was a lighter and faster tank with a road speed of 8.3mph. The tracks went round an armoured plated chassis, on top of and at the rear of which was a fighting turret. It was armed with four Hotchkiss light machine guns. (The right to manufacture these had been purchased for the Royal Small Arms factory from the French Hotchkiss Company.) The Whippet was intended for exploitation and for more open warfare; its role being more akin to that of the original light cavalry, whilst the Mark V undertook the function of the 'heavies'.[4]

But if opportunities for cavalry action were limited on the Western Front, it was far otherwise in Palestine. There General Allenby's great offensive in 1918 provided the only opportunity in the war, and probably the last in history, for the complete destruction of an army by the rapid advance of a mass of horsemen. A door was forced open in the enemy's lines, and as (to carry the metaphor further) it was pushed back on its hinges, a torrent of mounted troops poured through the opening. In six weeks they swept 400 miles deep into enemy territory. It was indeed a forerunner of the 1940 'blitzkrieg', except that it was carried out by horsemen instead of by tanks. The Desert Mounted Corps, with its four cavalry divisions, constituted one of the largest bodies of horse ever to operate tactically under one command.[5]

As a result of its success in Palestine, cavalry inevitably remained as an important element in the Army after the end of World War I. Nevertheless it was becoming clear that cavalry were destined to play a smaller part in the warfare of the future. Some regiments were amalgamated, and eventually it was only the small amount of money placed at the disposal of the Army which held up the re-equipment of most cavalry regiments with tanks or armoured cars instead of horses. In April 1939, a few months before the outbreak of World War II, cavalry regiments and the Royal Tank Regiment were grouped together to form the Royal Armoured Corps; though regiments retained their identities and their old names.

For those who foresaw the importance of the tank in a future conflict, the years between the two wars were a depressing period. Owing, presumably, to the lack of money for new equipment, there was a rudimentary organisation in the War Office for tank design, and only the pioneering of the firm of Vickers-Armstrong ensured some progress in the design and development of armoured fighting vehicles. Even in 1936 the Army had only 375 tanks (209 light and 166 medium), and of these 304 were considered obsolete.[6]

The production of tanks was stopped almost immediately after the Armistice of 1918. There had been a wartime development of the Whippet, or Medium Mark A, which was known as the Medium Mark B, and which had a heavier armament but was slower. Only 45 were built because of the advent of the much more effective Medium Mark C, or Hornet, designed in 1917. The hull was very similar in shape to that of the heavy tanks, but mounted on top at the front was a large fixed turret, surmounted by a small revolving turret for the commander. There were male and female varieties, the former having a 6-pounder gun in the fixed turret and three Hotchkiss light machine guns at the sides and back, and the latter four Hotchkiss LMGs. The road speed was 7.9mph. These tanks formed the main equipment of the Tank Corps after the war. On 28 April 1918 a conference was held at Tank Corps Headquarters to consider the specification for a still more advanced tank. It was decided that for deep penetration a speed of 20mph was required together with a radius of action of 200 miles. To meet this need an experimental medium tank was built as Mark D, with a speed of 18mph and a low hull, surmounted at the rear by a revolving turret.[7]

On 12 November 1918 instructions were issued that no more tanks were to be built except the new Mediums C and D. Of the former 500 were under construction, but only 36 were completed, the remainder being cancelled so that money should be available for the Medium Ds. Another experimental equipment, the Light Infantry Tank, underwent its first trials in September 1921. It could float and reached a maximum speed of 30mph. Both the Medium D and the Light Infantry tank were of such an advanced design that there were the inevitable 'teething' troubles. Rather than await the completion of the trials, the Master-General of the Ordnance ordered a medium tank from Messrs Vickers, and by December 1922 this had completed its trials satisfactorily. It was put into production at once, in order not to lose the money voted in the 1921-22 estimates for tank construction. As a result of this diversion of the available funds, further progress on two very promising tanks was halted.[8]

The Vickers Medium tank had a main armament of a 3-pounder gun in a revolving turret and a secondary armament of three Hotchkiss LMGs for close defence. The first production models reached the Army in 1924, and with their speed of 18mph they were noteworthy as being the first fast tanks to be issued to any army in the world. The Vickers remained the Army's principal tank until 1938. As a vehicle it was very reliable, and its steadiness resulted in a very high standard of gunnery.[9]

The first light tanks adopted by the Army were designed by the firm of Carden-Loyd; the Mark I of 1929 being a two-man vehicle mounting a Vickers machine gun in a rotating turret and having a speed of 32mph. Carden-Loyd were absorbed by the new combine of Vickers-Armstrong, and this firm built all the subsequent light tanks of this type. Marks II, III, and IV were very similar, but the Mark V of 1934 had a two-man, instead of a one-man, turret, and two Vickers machine guns mounted coaxially, a .5in and a .303in. The Mark V was rather too sensitive in its steering, and it was soon superseded by the Mark VI, which was the predominant light tank in the early campaigns of World War II. It was a good little tank for its intended role as a reconnaissance vehicle.[10]

In 1929 a series of experimental tanks were designed, classed as A7. Their armament consisted of two coaxial machine guns in a turret and a third in a gimbal in the hull. Three were built, of which the last, completed in 1936, had a much more powerful engine than the first two. From these three designs were developed the cruiser tanks of World War II.[11]

In 1931 the 1st Tank Brigade was formed from the four existing tank battalions, three of which were composed of both light and medium tanks and the fourth of light tanks only.[12]

In 1934 a replacement for the now obsolete Vickers Medium tank had still not been selected. It was decided, however, that instead of continuing with the current conception of a medium tank with the dual role of close support for the infantry and the main element in a mobile striking force, separate tanks should be designed for each of these roles. The former task was to be undertaken by a heavily armoured and rather slow 'Infantry' tank, as in 1916-1918, on a scale of one battalion for each infantry division. The main tank of the mobile armoured force was to be a development of the 'Whippet' idea, that is, fast with an armament equal to that of the infantry tank but much more lightly armoured. It was to be called a 'Cruiser'; though a more accurate naval analogy for

the two tanks would have been that of Battle tank and Battle Cruiser tank.

The new policy led to the design of a number of different types of cruiser tank and three types of infantry tank before the outbreak of World War II. The infantry tanks were to be the equipment of Army Tank battalions, whilst the cruiser tanks were to be the main armoured fighting vehicles of the new armoured divisions. (In 1938 the 1st Tank Brigade and some mechanised cavalry regiments were formed into the Mobile Division, which in 1939 was renamed the Armoured Division.) Yet when war came in September 1939 the 1st Armoured Division was still without its cruiser tanks, and only two army tank battalions had been equipped with infantry tanks.[13]

When the British Expeditionary Force sailed for France in 1939 the divisional cavalry regiments were equipped with the Vickers Mark VI light tanks. These were the regiments intended to carry out the cavalry role of reconnaissance and protection — the 4th/7th and 5th Dragoon Guards, the 13th/18th and 15th/19th Hussars, the 1st Lothian and Border Horse, the Fife and Forfar Yeomanry, and the East Riding Yeomanry. Directly under GHQ there was an armoured car regiment, the 12th Lancers, for long distance reconnaissance, which led the BEF in the advance into Belgium. There was the 1st Army Tank Brigade, but it consisted of only two battalions, the 4th Royal Tank Regiment, and the 7th Royal Tank Regiment; the former being equipped with Mark I infantry tanks and the latter with Mark Is and Mark IIs, in approximately equal numbers. The Mark Is were the original 'Matildas', so-called by General Sir Hugh Elles, the MGO, because of their fancied resemblance to a contemporary cartoon comic duck of that name. Their maximum speed was 8mph and they were armed with only one machine gun of either .303in or .5in calibre. Their principal feature was the thick armour of 65mm in front and 60mm on the sides. The Mark IIs (which later inherited the name 'Matilda') were much better tanks, armed with a 2-pounder gun and a 7.92mm Besa machine gun. Their armour plate had a maximum thickness of 75mm, making them the most heavily armoured tanks in the world. (The Besa machine gun was a British modification of the Czech ZB vz53, manufactured by the Birmingham Small Arms Company from 1939 in the original calibre to avoid trouble in converting it to .303in.)[14]

The number of heavily armoured tanks was therefore very small, but if it had not been for these two battalions the BEF would have probably been surrounded and forced to surrender, with the likely loss of the war as a consequence. By 21 May the German armoured divisions, which had broken through the French Ninth Army about Sedan, had reached the Channel coast and were turning north. On that same day a British counter-attack was launched in the Arras area by a small force, spearheaded by the 4th and 7th Royal Tanks, which, after long moves on tracks, had only 58 Mark Is and 16 Mark IIs serviceable between them. As it happened this attack began an hour before the German General Rommel planned to attack with his own 7th Armoured Division, with the SS Totenkopf Division advancing on his left and the 5th Armoured Division co-operating on his right. The advancing British armour caught the Germans 'on the wrong foot'. The first brunt of the attack fell on the motorised infantry of the 7th Armoured Division and on the SS Division; part of the latter panicked and fled. The Germans found to their dismay that their anti-tank guns were useless against the armour of the infantry tanks; one Matilda receiving 14 direct hits from 37mm guns without effect. Rommel said that his guns were destroyed by fire or overrun, and that their crews were almost annihilated. He thought, indeed, that he was being attacked by tanks in superior strength to his own, and referred in his report to 'hundreds of enemy tanks and following infantry'. This implies that he estimated the British strength to be at least two armoured divisions. Bad news gathers strength as it travels, and the German higher command envisaged a massive British counter-stroke which threatened to cut off and immobilise the bulk of their own armour. Hence the advance of the German tanks was checked, and the 1st and 2nd Armoured Divisons were pulled back in case of any further threat from the Arras area. The remaining armoured divisions were halted on 24 May, first by Field Marshal von Runstedt, commanding Army Group A, and then by a confirmatory order from Hitler himself, after he had visited von Runstedt's headquarters.[15]

When World War II started there were few horse soldiers left in the British Army. The last horsed cavalry regiments of the Regular Army were mechanised in 1940, and there remained only the 5th Cavalry Brigade of three Yeomanry regiments, the Cheshire Yeomanry, the North Somerset Yeomanry, and the Yorkshire Dragoons. In June 1941 British forces had the unwelcome task of taking the field against their former allies in Syria, who were serving under the French Vichy

Government. Two regiments of the 5th Cavalry Brigade, the Cheshire, or Earl of Chester's, Yeomanry, and the Queen's Own Yorkshire Dragoons, served right through the Syrian campaign and are the last mounted units of the British Army to have served in action as such.[16]

The 'see-saw' battles of the Western Desert provided a most interesting testing period for successive designs of tank used by the British Army. In 1940 the 7th Armoured Division was equipped with cruiser tanks and light tanks, of which the latter provided by far the greater proportion. The cruiser tanks were of two varieties, the Mark I and the Mark II. The Mark I had a speed of 23mph and was armed with a 2-pounder gun and a coaxially mounted Vickers machine gun in the main turret, and with two other Vickers guns, one in each of two smaller turrets in the forward part of the vehicle. The Mark II was, with a speed of 16mph, considerably slower. It did not have the subsidiary machine gun turrets, but its armour was proof against .5in armour-piercing ammunition, whilst the Mark I's armour only protected it against ordinary small arms fire. Of the two the Mark II was the better and more reliable tank. In August 1940 three regiments were sent from England as reinforcements, of which one was equipped with light tanks, one with Infantry tanks Mark II (now Matildas), and one with Cruiser tanks Marks II and III. The Mark III had Christie suspension, thicker armour and a speed of 20mph. Thus reinforced, the 7th Armoured Division and the 7th Royal Tank Regiment (with the Matildas) were the principal elements in O'Connor's Western Desert Force which destroyed the Italian army attempting to invade Egypt.[17]

More tank reinforcements were sent from England after Rommel's successful offensive in the spring of 1941. Amongst these were the new Mark VI Cruisers, named 'Crusaders', with a Christie suspension, a speed of 27mph, 40mm maximum armour thickness, a 2-pounder gun, two Besa machine guns, and a Bren gun in an anti-aircraft mounting. Some of the Crusaders, intended for close support, had 3in howitzers instead of 2-pounder guns. The Crusader was fast and manoeuvrable with an excellent suspension, but it was not mechanically very reliable and it was under-gunned. Nevertheless it remained the standard tank of the 7th Armoured Division until the battle of El Alamein.[18]

By the summer of 1941 Valentine infantry tanks had arrived in the Middle East. The Valentine was the last British tank to be designed before the outbreak of war. It ran into 11 different marks, and was used in North Africa until 1943. The Mark I had 65mm armour, a maximum speed of 15mph, an armament of a 2-pounder gun and a Besa machine gun. Marks VIII-X had a 6-pounder gun and the Mark XI a 75mm gun. Marks II and onwards had diesel engines instead of petrol.[19]

The light tanks in the Middle East were replaced about this time by the American 'Stuart', or 'Honey', armed with a 37mm gun and a coaxially mounted .30in Browning machine gun in a turret and another Browning in the hull. It had a speed of 36mph, but a rather limited range of 70 miles.[20]

By the beginning of 1942 the American 'Grant' medium tank had been issued to some of the British armoured regiments. The main armament of the Grant was a 75mm gun, mounted in a sponson on the right side of the hull, as no suitable turret was available for it. As a secondary armament a 37mm gun was mounted in a turret of British design. It had a speed of 26mph, a radius of action of 144 miles and 57mm thick armour plating. The mounting of the 75mm gun was a grave handicap, as not only did it have a very limited traverse, but it could not be used at all when the tank was 'hull down'. The first major conflict in which the Grants were engaged was the disastrous battle of Gazala, when Rommel defeated the British Eighth Army and drove it back to the Egyptian frontier in June 1942.[21]

Before Montgomery's victory at El Alamein in October 1942 the Eighth Army had received American medium tanks of a new type, the 'Sherman'. The armament consisted of a 75mm gun and co-axially mounted Browning machine gun in a turret and another Browning in the hull. The maximum armour thickness was 76mm, and the tank had a speed of 24mph and a range of 85 miles.[22] The total number of British tanks in the forthcoming battle was 1,080, of which 270 were Shermans and 210 Grants. Also included were Crusaders armed with 6-pounder guns. A notable incident of the battle was the gallant charge by the 9th Armoured Brigade to force a gap through the enemy anti-tank screen. The Brigade lost 87 tanks, but Montgomery had told its commander that the forcing of this gap was of such importance that he must be prepared for 100% casualties.[23]

In June 1941 the first production models of a new infantry tank, the Mark IV, appeared. It was known as the 'Churchill' and first went into action at the attack on Dieppe in August 1942. Three of them were tested at Alamein, and later they were very popular in close country

during the campaign in Tunisia. The first Churchills had a frontal armour 100mm thick, but the 2-pounder gun in the turret of this 38½ ton vehicle rather gave the impression of an elephant armed with a pea-shooter. In March 1942 a start was made in replacing the 2-pounder with a 6-pounder, and 120 of those used in Tunisia were modified to take the 75mm guns fitted in the Shermans. So modified, they were known as 'NA 75s'. The Churchill's maximum speed was 15½mph and it had a range of 90 miles.[24]

Most of the tanks with which the British armoured divisions were equipped for the invasion of Normandy were Shermans equipped with 17-pounder guns and known as 'Fireflies', but all the armoured reconnaissance regiments of the armoured divisions had a new medium tank of British design called the 'Cromwell'. It was one of the fastest tanks in the war; and originally too fast for its Christie suspension, so that in later models the maximum speed was geared down to 32mph. Its maximum thickness of armour was 76mm, though in some later welded models this was increased to 101mm. The earliest marks had one 6-pounder gun and two Besa machine guns. It was soon realised that the gun was too light and Marks IV, V, and VII were armed with a medium velocity 75mm gun — inferior, however, to the latest German tank gun of this calibre. Marks VI and VIII were for close support and were armed with 95mm howitzers. The range of the Cromwell was 165 miles.

To increase the firepower of an armoured regiment a modified Cromwell was produced, named the 'Challenger', with the same speed but armed with a 17-pounder (76.2mm) gun and coaxially mounted .30in machine gun, and having armour 102mm thick. A few were used in North-West Europe, but their performance was disappointing, in spite of a good gun.

So far tanks mounting 17-pounder guns had been modified from existing types, but now a new tank, the 'Comet', was designed especially to carry a 17-pounder. This was actually a modification of the existing 17-pounder and was officially called a 77mm. In action it proved to be a good and accurate gun. The Comet had a speed of 25mph, a range of 123 miles, and an all-welded hull with armour 101mm thick at the maximum. It was not, however, until after the crossing of the Rhine that the Comet first went into action, when it soon showed itself to be the finest British tank of the war.[25]

One very important addition to the British tank armoury was the swimming, or 'Duplex-Drive' (DD) tank. Some hundreds of Shermans were so converted for the invasion of Europe. The term 'duplex-drive' meant that the tank was fitted with a propeller at the rear, powered by the tank's bevel drive. Round the hull there was a deck to which was attached the bottom of a canvas screen. When raised by compressed air this formed a hull from which the tank was suspended in the water. Once the tank reached the shore the screen could be collapsed and it could drive straight into action.[26]

The pursuit by the British armoured divisions after victory in the stubborn Normandy operations was reminiscent of Allenby's cavalry pursuit in Palestine. It started on 17 August; on 3 September the Guards Armoured Division entered Brussels, on the same day the 11th Armoured Division seized Antwerp, and on 5 September the 7th Armoured Division captured Ghent. These divisions had covered 230 miles in seven days, an average of over 30 miles a day.

In 1945, just too late to take part in the war, issue began of a new British tank. It was called the 'Centurion' and it was undoubtedly at that time the finest armoured fighting vehicle in existence. It weighed 50 ton, as compared with the 32½ of the Comet, but had a slower speed than the latter (22mph) and its maximum armour thickness was less (76mm). The early models had the same 17-pounder gun as the Sherman Firefly, but the Mark III of 1948 had a 20-pounder gun, and in 1959 the 105mm gun was fitted. Centurions first went into action in the Korean campaign of 1950, where they proved their value, and they have distinguished themselves subsequently in the service of foreign countries which have purchased them. In 1954 armoured regiments were given greater firepower with the arrival of the largest and heaviest tanks in existence — the 65 ton heavily armoured 'Conqueror', armed with a 120mm gun. The purpose was to provide fire support for the Centurion by engaging enemy heavy tanks and self-propelled guns. In addition to its 120mm gun the Conqueror had two machine guns, one coaxially mounted, and the other in the cupola for anti-aircraft fire. The speed was 22mph.[27]

The Royal Armoured Corps, like the Infantry, suffered reductions in strength with the disappearance of Imperial responsibilities. Like the Infantry, this was effected partly by amalgamations. In the Appendix are listed the successive amalgamations and alterations of title which have occurred in cavalry regiments from the latter part of the 19th century onwards.

3

Artillery

When the Boer War broke out in 1899, the British field artillery was outmoded both in equipment and practice. This was due principally to the type of enemy which the Army had had to fight during the latter part of the 19th century. The rate of fire was slow because of the time taken up by the recoil of the gun carriage after each shot. There was an additional factor, in that, if a favourable wind was lacking, time had to be allowed for the smoke caused by the black powder to clear before a piece could be fired again.

The problem of increasing the rate of artillery fire was examined by General Wille of the German Army and Colonel Langlois of the French Army in 1891. They both maintained that it was not possible to increase the rate of fire unless the recoil of a piece after firing could be absorbed. This argument led to the development of a non-recoiling carriage which remained in position after firing, whilst the piece itself slid backwards under the control of a hydraulic buffer and was pressed back into place by a spring recuperator.[1] Rapid fire entailed, too, the use of a smokeless powder and a metal cartridge case, so that a fresh charge could be loaded with safety immediately after firing without sponging or washing out. A metal cartridge case had the additional advantage of incorporating its own means of ignition, thereby avoiding the removal of the old and the insertion of a fresh primer. The term 'Quick Firing' (QF) thus came to be applied to an equipment having a metal cartridge case to contain the charge and seal the gas, whether the ammunition was fixed (ie projectile fixed to the cartridge case) or separate; whereas 'Breech Loading' (BL) implied an equipment which used bags to contain the charge and in which the sealing was effected by fixing a pad to the breech screw.[2]

But in 1891 it was the prevailing British opinion that rapid fire by field artillery would be required only on rare occasions, such as a cavalry attack on battery positions or the appearance of a fleeting target. The metal cartridge case was of limited value as an aid to rapid fire unless used in conjunction with a full recoil carriage and smokeless powder, and there was the disadvantage that the permissible loads carried by gun limbers and ammunition wagons would entail a reduction in the number of rounds owing to the weight of the metal cases. A recoil carriage was in fact designed in 1881 and taken into limited use by the Royal Artillery in 1891; but the compression of springs in a recoil cylinder only allowed a movement of about four inches, which was insufficient to absorb the full recoil and it had to be supplemented by a self-acting tyre-brake.[3]

In 1881 a 12-pounder rifled breech loading (RBL) gun was adopted for both the Royal Horse Artillery and the Royal Field Artillery. It proved too heavy for the RHA, however, and was soon superseded by a lighter equipment of the same calibre. It was retained by the RFA but was converted in 1894 into a 15-pounder. The carriage recoil of these equipments was controlled by a spade and spring arrangement, whereby a spade below the axletree was forced into the ground by the recoil and springs in the trail returned the carriage to the firing position. Some equipments had the short recoil carriage mentioned above.

Guns were normally sited in the open because they were not equipped to shoot and hit from behind cover. But, employed against the Boers, this practice led to heavy casualties, particularly as shields could not be fitted to provide protection on gun carriages that recoiled. The new smokeless explosives allowed guns to be concealed, but, if hidden behind cover, they could no longer fire over open sights. A new system of sighting was therefore needed urgently, and to meet this need an

arrangement known as the 'Gunner's Arc' was improvised. The foresight was replaced by a strip of wood fastened at right angles to the piece, with holes bored into it at half-degree intervals. The centre hole was in the same position as the old foresight, and into this was stuck a match stick. An aiming point was selected on the crest of the hill or rise in front, approximately in line with the target, and the sights were aligned on it. An observer was placed where he could see the enemy's position. When the gun was fired the observer would, if necessary, give a correction in the form of, say, 'left three degrees'. The match stick would then be moved six holes to the right and the sights re-aligned on the aiming point. It was a remarkably successful system.[4]

The field artillery also had the 5in BL howitzer, and the medium and heavy artillery equipments were, respectively, the 4.75in QF gun (using metal cartridge cases but without a full recoil carriage), the 6in BL howitzer, and the 9.45 BL howitzer.[5]

The Boers had some 75mm QF rifled guns, made in 1896 by the firm Canet, Schneider of Creusot, which compared well with British field equipments. They had hydraulic buffers which allowed a recoil of $11\frac{1}{2}$ inches and two cylinders with spiral springs to restore the piece to position, supplemented by spade and springs on the carriage. The charge of smokeless powder was contained in a metal case separated from the shell. The rate of fire was reported to be from eight to ten rounds a minute.[6]

It was clear that British field artillery was not up to modern requirements, particularly as it was reported that the French field artillery had been equipped with a QF gun firing more than 20 rounds a minute (the famous 75mm). While the Boer War was still being waged the Director-General of Ordnance, General Sir Henry Brackenbury, was directed to advise on the re-equipment of the Royal Artillery. Brackenbury recommended that the whole of the existing equipment should be replaced within three years, and, this having been accepted, he began his investigation into ways of doing it. He had a clear idea of the type of equipment needed, but no British firm could design and manufacture it in sufficient quantities within the three years stipulated. However, he found that a German firm in Dusseldorf was manufacturing a remarkable QF field gun designed by an engineer named Ehrhardt. It was a 15-pounder with a long-recoil top carriage and it could equal the rate of fire of the new French gun. Brackenbury immediately ordered sufficient equipment for 18 batteries. The main feature of the equipment was the cradle with hydraulic buffer and spring recuperator. When, some time later, the RFA received British designed equipment, these Ehrhardt batteries were handed over to the Territorial Army and to some units overseas.[7]

In 1903 four batteries were equipped with two types of QF gun, a 13-pounder and an 18-pounder, which had been designed jointly by British firms. After successful trials, the RHA got the 13-pounder and the RFA the 18-pounder; all the Regular divisions being equipped with the new guns by 1906. They were of identical design; the piece recoiled, sliding on the guide ribs, and was checked by a hydraulic buffer placed above the gun and surrounded by metal recuperating springs. They were very accurate and could be fired at a rate of 20 aimed rounds a minute. The gunners were protected by a bullet proof shield. Only shrapnel ammunition was supplied at this stage. Before the end of 1914, however, some high explosive shell was supplied and tried, and it became so popular that eventually half of the ammunition for these guns was HE.[8]

It was not till 1914, shortly before the outbreak of war, that the Royal Artillery had a QF field howitzer. This excellent and very accurate piece was of 4.5in calibre. Its ammunition was at first 70% shrapnel and 30% HE, but the use of shrapnel was stopped very early in World War I.[9]

An artillery surprise of the South African War had been the heavy guns of the Boer Army, and in 1902 a committee was set up to select a new heavy (or really medium) equipment. They chose a promising 60-pounder BL gun which had been designed by the firm of Armstrong as a speculative venture. After tests this was approved and in 1906 a four-gun 60-pounder battery of the royal Garrison Artillery was allotted to each infantry division. Ammunition was again 70% shrapnel and 30% HE.[10]

No real thought had as yet been given to the provision of really heavy equipments, except for a solitary order for a prototype 9.2in howitzer from Vickers, which was delivered in June 1914. (A scale model of this impressive weapon is incorporated in the Royal Artillery memorial at Hyde Park Corner.) There was no immediate order for production, because a replacement for the Boer War 6in 30cwt howitzer was considered more urgent. The answer was found in a 6in 26cwt howitzer which was designed in a few weeks and was in production by autumn 1915 (an interesting comparison with the time required from the stated requirement to the production of any modern equipment!). For the first time there was a Schneider pattern air recuperator, as used on the French 75mm field gun, and this in due course replaced the spring recuperators on the 13-pounders and 18-pounders. The new piece became the standard medium howitzer, and by the end of the war 1,246 had been issued to the Royal Artillery and another 212 to Allied armies.[11]

In 1915 production started of the Mark II version of the Mark I, or prototype, 9.2in howitzer, and 450 were eventually manufactured. In the same year a 12in howitzer was designed and produced, which followed as far as possible the plan for the 9.2in, in order to save time. An 8in howitzer, on the lines of the 6in, followed in 1917. The biggest guns used on the Western Front were the 12in and 14in pieces on railway mountings. For anti-aircraft fire an excellent weapon was designed — a 3in 20cwt QF gun on a high angle mounting, which was used either for static defence or, secured to a lorry-towed platform, for mobile operations.[12]

The fighting on the Western Front has been well-styled a 'gunner's war', for there was a bigger concentration of ordnance than ever before or since, and, with the advent of guided missiles, it is unlikely that such a vast quantity will ever be used again. Although, when operations started, the emphasis was on field artillery, it was increasingly the heavy artillery that came to play the major role in this predominantly siege warfare. The heavy howitzer was the most useful weapon because only its shells were really effective against parapets and deep dug-outs. Field artillery was engaged primarily in wire-cutting. At the battle of Messines in May 1917 the Royal Artillery had 2,266 pieces of ordnance, of which 756 were heavy, giving one of the latter to every 20 yards of front.

The standard practice at this time was to blast the enemy position with an avalanche of fire for days on end, using shells from dumps that it had taken weeks to stock. At the end of this bombardment the infantry advanced to assault, under a creeping barrage; that is to say, a curtain of artillery fire which moved forward by periodic lifts at roughly the pace of the advancing infantry. Surprise was inevitably lost, and it was only the eventual possession of tanks in large numbers that allowed this long preliminary bombardment to be dispensed with and the possibility of surprise restored.

Throughout World War I all the field artillery was drawn by horses, and even the 60-pounders were so pulled, generally by heavy Clydesdales. By 1915, however, mechanical traction was being used for the massive howitzers. After the war, and until the 1930s, the guns and howitzers of horse and field artillery were still drawn by six-horse teams. The gradual change to mechanical traction was started by replacing the team of horses with their limber, by a motor truck. However, the conventional four-wheeled motor trucks had not nearly the cross-country capacity of horses. A compromise was sought at first by using a truck to tow a gun along a road, and having carried on or pulled by the same truck a small tractor to draw the piece across country. This cumbersome arrangement was replaced by the fully tracked 'Dragon' (ie 'drag-gun') and the four-wheeled drive 'Ant'. Tracks were not suited for long road movement and six-wheeled vehicles eventually became standard for towing. Rubber tyres for gun carriages followed, and by 1939 all British artillery was mechanically drawn.[13]

In January 1917 there had been the first trial of a self-propelled equipment, known as a 'Gun-Carrying Tank'. A 60-pounder gun and a 6in howitzer, with carriage wheels removed, were mounted on the chassis of Mark I tanks. Although they could be fired from their tracked mounting, they were normally refitted with their wheels (which were carried on the outside of the tank chassis) and fired in the usual way. This experiment was not continued, but in 1924 Vickers designed and built some self-propelled equipments, using a chassis of the same type as their medium tank on which was mounted an 18-pounder gun. A number were tried on manoeuvres the following year, but most military opinion was against them.[14]

In 1924 the Royal Artillery was reorganised. The distinction that had existed between the Royal Garrison Artillery (Heavy, Coast, and Pack) on the one hand, and the Royal Horse Artillery and Royal Field Artillery on the other, disappeared, and the Royal Artillery was reconstituted as one Regiment. In 1938 there was a further reorganisation. The Regiment was divided into two branches, one being field artillery and the other comprising coast defence, anti-aircraft and anti-tank artillery. The term 'brigade' was replaced by 'regiment' to designate a unit of artillery and there were alterations in the organisation and number of batteries in it.

The rapid development in the speed and height of aircraft led to the provision of new anti-aircraft guns with improved appliances and high muzzle velocity. These were the 40mm Bofors light anti-aircraft gun, and the 3.7in and 4.5in QF heavy anti-aircraft guns.

In the early 1930s a requirement arose for a field gun firing a heavier shell than the 18-pounder with a greater range. Trials were carried out with various equipments and a 3.45in piece firing a 25lb shell was selected. It was to be an all-purpose field equipment, replacing the 13-pounder gun, the 18-pounder gun, and the 4.5in howitzer, and having HE ammunition only with variable charges. (The decision to do without shrapnel was due to the improved fragmentation of the latest common HE shell.) The prototype underwent trials between 1935 and 1937. Production was held up by the lack of money, and it was not till 1939 that these 25-pounder QF gun-howitzers, as they were termed, were issued to the Royal Artillery. Fixed ammunition was abandoned in order that charges could be adjusted to the type of target engaged. The variety of charges allowed for a steep angle of descent when needed, and it was this attribute which caused the piece to be called a gun-howitzer. A number of other new artillery equipments had also been delayed for the same reason. Of these, the 5.5in BL medium gun-howitzer had been designed to replace the 6in 26cwt howitzer. It became notable for its mobility, range, and power, and proved particularly effective against Japanese bunkers in Burma. The 60-pounder gun was replaced by a 4.5in BL medium gun, and a 7.2in BL heavy howitzer replaced the 8in and 9.2in howitzers. The prototype of the 5.5in gun-howitzer was tried in 1938, but issue to the Royal Artillery had not started when World War II broke out. It had rear trunnions to allow for recoil and, since this made it muzzle heavy, there were two nearly vertical spring equilibrators to compensate for this, a characteristic feature of the piece. The first 4.5in guns, which came out about the same time, were relined 60-pounders, though later marks were new pieces. The gun was mounted on the same carriage as the 5.5in, incorporating the rear trunnion cradle and equilibrators. The 7.2in howitzer did not arrive till 1941.[15]

The first anti-tank guns, 2-pounders, were delivered in 1937. By the spring of 1941 Rommel's first advance in the Western Desert led to a demand from Headquarters Middle East Command for large numbers of bigger anti-tank guns. A 6-pounder gun had been conceived before the war and was ready for trial early in 1940. In the early part of the war, however, the 2-pounder had been satisfactory against the armour of the time and in the first Libyan campaign had proved better than the German 37mm. No priority was given, therefore, for the construction of 6-pounders, in case the delivery of 2-pounders should thereby be slowed down. Initial production in response to the Middle East demand was therefore slow and it was not till the spring of 1942 that 6-pounders were reaching the Army in quantity. The 6-pounder was an excellent weapon, better even than the famed German Pak 38. It was succeeded in its turn by the 17-pounder, which reached North Africa in time to tackle the formidable German Tiger tank during the final stages of the campaign.[16]

Improvised self-propelled ordnance was first provided in the Middle East by mounting a 25-pounder on a Valentine tank chassis. By the battle of Alamein, however, an American equipment had reached the Eighth Army in some numbers. This was the 105mm 'Howitzer Motor Carriage M7', which incorporated the M2 medium tank chassis. With this as a model, the British Sexton equipment was designed, using the Canadian Ram medium tank chassis as a mount for a 25-pounder. Later on a 17-pounder was mounted on a Valentine tank to provide the Archer self-propelled anti-tank gun.[17]

4

Engineers

In the British Army the Corps of Royal Engineers is unique as regards the number and variety of the tasks it has been called upon to undertake, and the activities which it has started but which have subsequently become separate arms of the Service or been transferred to other arms. Signal communications were perhaps the largest of such activities, but from its start the Royal Engineer Signal Service (which eventually became the Royal Corps of Signals) was virtually a separate branch, and it is dealt with in the next chapter.

The vast area over which the Boer War was fought resulted in a great expansion of field engineering, with bridging and demolitions playing a major part in the work of the Corps. Field troops and field companies became increasingly valuable components of cavalry and infantry divisions respectively, and the Royal Engineers' part in the operation and maintenance of railways was vital to the flow of supplies over the long lines of communication. During the guerilla operations of the later stages of the war, Kitchener's network of garrisoned blockhouses, wire, and protective camps were built by the Sappers.[1]

After the end of the Boer War the increased importance of railways was recognised by the formation in 1905 of a Railway Training Centre from the original two Royal engineer railway companies.

In 1911 military flying was officially established with the formation of the Air Battalion RE. This was not an activity that remained with the Sappers for very long, for the following year the Air Battalion was disbanded on the formation of the Royal Flying Corps.[2]

During the years 1914 to 1918, on the Western Front the Royal Engineers were faced with a long period of siege warfare for the first time since the Crimea, but in tackling the numerous problems that arose, they were never in such desperate straits for men and equipment as in the earlier conflict. As the troops settled down to trench fighting, so the divisional field companies dealt with such miscellaneous needs as periscopes, grenades, trench mortars, pumps and camouflage screens. Roads, tracks, and light railways were constructed for the movement of men, equipment, and supplies over ground which had often been turned into cratered mud by the heavy shelling. Tunnelling companies built long galleries in their mining operations beneath the enemy lines — operations that culminated in the destruction of the German defences on the Messines-Wytschaete ridge, by the vast explosion of a mass of linked mines 100 feet below the surface. To achieve this outstanding success, officers and men had worked for two years without being detected by an alert and suspicious enemy.

Some 34 million maps of various kinds were produced by the RE survey companies. The survey battalions with each Army issued a new situation map nearly every day; and large scale plans were prepared for the artillery, fixing the positions of guns and targets for barrages and for the accurate unregistered shelling which was such an essential element in the surprise achieved at the decisive battle of Amiens in August 1918.[3]

Some of the extent of RE work on the Western Front can be gathered from the engineer units in the Fourth Army at the opening of the battle of Amiens on 8 August 1918. In addition to those belonging to corps and divisions, there were three gas (projector) companies, two gas (mortar) companies, one field company, 11 army troops companies, two siege companies, seven tunnelling companies, one electrical and mechanical company, one water boring section, one army workshops company, one field survey battalion with five sound ranging sections and four observation groups, two foreway companies for tramways, one barge infiltration unit, two advanced RE parks, three forestry units, one army printing advanced section, and one advanced photographic section.[4] It will be noted from the above that gas was a RE function, and indeed at the battle of Loos on 25 September 1915 the Special Brigade RE delivered the first British gas attack.[5]

Ports, coastal craft, railways, and inland water transport were the responsibility of the RE Transportation and Movement Control Service. By 1917 130 RE companies with a total strength of over 100,000 men were operating, constructing, and repairing docks, harbours, railways, bridges, and inland waterways. (This responsibility was retained by the Royal Engineers until it was handed over to the Royal Corps of Transport in 1965.)[6]

In the Middle East the army advancing into Palestine was followed across the Sinai desert by RE companies building a pipe carrying water from the Nile and a standard gauge railway, side by side. In the United Kingdom RE units manned 285 anti-aircraft searchlights, organised into 95 sections each of three lights.[7]

In common with other arms, the Royal Engineers suffered between the two World Wars from the lack of money made available to the fighting Services. In 1920, for instance, the 1st Searchlight Battalion RE had a cadre strength of only one officer and seven other ranks. By 1938, however, the all too belated expansion of the Army and the priority given to air defence had resulted in the swelling of this token element to 26 anti-aircraft searchlight battalions. The searchlight component of air defence did not remain a Royal Engineer responsibility for very long, for in the early stages of World War II it was logically transferred to the Royal Artillery.[8]

There was progress in bridging equipment during this interwar period. The Small Box Girder bridge was produced to carry the 20 ton Vickers Medium tank over a gap of up to 64ft. Later it was strengthened to bear the weight of the heavier Infantry Tank Mark I, or Matilda. This bridge was the forerunner of most modern military bridging equipment, as it was the first to be pinned together rather than bolted. During the latter part of World War II it was chosen for the Assault Vehicle RE (AVRE) bridgelayer. The Small Box Girder was followed by the Large Box Girder and Hamilton bridges for heavier loads.[9]

In World War II the Corps of Royal Engineers was probably of greater proportionate importance on the battlefield than ever before in its history.

In 1939 the 'Class' system of vehicles and bridges was introduced. Bridges were marked from 5 to 40, according to the loads they could carry, and similar numbers were painted on the front mudguards of vehicles to show the lowest numbered bridge over which they could be driven.

There was a notable advance in field bridging. Mr R. A. Riddles,

Deputy Director of Royal Engineer Equipment, experienced difficulty in getting a bridge which he considered suitable. Mr D. Bailey, chief designer at the Experimental Bridging Establishment, Christchurch, made a sketch for a suggested bridge on the back of a foolscap envelope. This was shown to Riddles, who liked the idea and approved the construction of a trial bridge. Trials were successful, the bridge was adopted, and Riddles was asked what it should be called. 'Well', he said, 'we already have the Hamilton and the Inglis; I think we should call this the Bailey'. The bridge was built up with a number of easily handled panels, pinned together, which could be added to longitudinally for extra length, and by 'storeys', or parallel trusses, for extra strength. Demand was so great that production was eventually astronomical.[10]

The summer of 1940 saw the birth of a small organisation, known as Ministry of Defence I, under Major Millis Jefferis RE, which produced an extraordinary range of new weapons, including the PIAT anti-tank mortar, the Limpet mine, the W bomb to be floated down the Rhine, booby traps, and sundry unconventional devices. It was not initially favoured by the Ministry of Supply, but Churchill's strong support was obtained, and with it the nickname of 'Winston Churchill's Toyshop'.[11]

Also in summer 1940 Lieutenant-Colonel J. F. Rock RE, with no previous air experience, was directed to organise an Army airborne unit of parachutists and gliderborne troops. As a result he formed and commanded the Glider Pilot Regiment — yet another activity fathered by this versatile Corps.[12]

During the war artillery survey was in the main transferred from the Royal Engineers to the Royal Artillery, except for the main triangulation. Bomb disposal became an important duty, and 120 mobile bomb disposal sections were formed. Even more important was the development of the capacity to construct roads and airfields rapidly, using mechanical equipment.[13]

The Royal Engineers played a distinguished part in the second battle of Alamein. Following the leading infantry and supported by tanks and artillery, they cleared lanes through thick belts of minefields and destroyed knocked-out enemy tanks before they could be recovered by the enemy. On the front of the 1st and 10th Armoured Divisions alone, over a width of up to 1,500 yards, some half dozen lanes, each 16 yards broad, were cleared through two or more enemy minefields, each about 400 yards deep. In this magnificent operation the Royal Engineers used a device called a Scorpion, which consisted of a flail mounted on the front of a tank to thrash the mine-strewn ground.[14]

The Scorpion heralded a number of specialised armoured vehicles which were used with such success at the Normandy landings and after by the Royal Armoured Corps and the Assault Royal Engineers. A special Tunnelling Training and Development Centre RE had been formed in 1941, and one of the results of its work was the Armoured Vehicle Royal Engineers (AVRE), which was a Churchill tank Mark IV, fitted in place of its gun with a 12in spigot mortar firing a 25lb shaped explosive (nicknamed a Dustbin) over a distance of up to 80 yards to break down concrete obstacles and defences. An AVRE could, in addition, carry one of the following: a large brushwood fascine for dropping to fill an anti-tank ditch, a 20ft tank assault (Small Box Girder) bridge, explosive 'Snakes' and 'Congers' to clear a path through a minefield, 'Bull's Horn' ploughs to sweep mines aside if it was desired to avoid cratering, or bobbins wound with coir matting and steel mesh track to lay crossings over the soft blue clay which would be encountered on certain beaches. The Scorpion had been developed into the Crab, which was a Sherman tank fitted with a flail, and which was now manned and operated by the Royal Armoured Corps. A Crocodile was a Churchill tank Mark VII fitted with a hull flame gun as well as its normal turret gun, and towing a trailer with 400gal of flame-thrower fuel and a nitrogen pressure system. An Ark consisted of a Churchill hull with a bridge on it back for climbing a wall or crossing a deep ditch. There were also armoured bulldozers. This specialised armour led the infantry into the attack in the invasion of Normandy, and it was a major factor in the speed with which the beaches were secured.[15]

In August 1944 the 5th Assault Regiment RE exchanged their AVREs for Buffaloes — officially, Landing Vehicles Tracked (LVT). There were two types, the Mark 2 which carried 24 passengers and had no ramp, and the Mark 4 which had a stern ramp and which could carry a 25-pounder, a jeep, a Bren carrier, or any similar load. Both had a water speed of 5mph and a land speed of 11mph. The 6th Assault Regiment RE and the 11th Royal Tank Regiment were also equipped with Buffaloes, but one squadron of the former had Terrapins — eight-wheeled amphibians.[16]

During the Scheldt operations in October 1944, 100 Buffaloes manned by the 5th ARRE and 42 Terrapins manned by the 6th ARRE were allocated to the 5th Canadian Infantry Brigade. Two assaulting columns were formed, one carrying the North Nova Scotia Highlanders and the other the Highland Light Infantry of Canada. Later lifts ferried the Brigade reserve and supplies. This was the first tactical use of Buffaloes and Terrapins in this theatre of war, and they carried successfully two infantry brigades, including 600 vehicles and guns.[17]

The 6th Assault Regiment RE figured again in the assault at Westkapelle, Walcheren. Two commandos led the attack, No 48 Commando in the Buffaloes of 82 Assault Squadron and No 41 Commando in those of 26 Assault Squadron. Following in reserve was No 47 Commando in 80 Assault Squadron's Buffaloes, while in those of 77 Assault Squadron were brigade headquarters and administrative units.[18] This very gallant operation provides a fitting finale to this brief account of the Royal Engineers.

5

Signals

Signalling arrived comparatively recently on the battlefield, because it was not till the increased range and accuracy of firepower drove units and formations too far apart for orders and reports to be conveyed by word of mouth, or even quickly enough by mounted messenger, that other more rapid means of communication had to be found. The means chosen were line telegraphy and visual signalling with flag, heliograph, and lamp. Originally it was intended that both line and visual should be the responsibility of one directorate, but by 1875 the Royal Engineers, the parents of signalling, had stopped using the latter, which now came under an Inspector of Army Signalling and was practised by officers and other ranks of cavalry and infantry. In 1886 the School of Signalling was formed to teach visual only, while telegraphy was absorbed into the Electrical wing of the School of Military Engineering.[1]

The first major test for the Telegraph Battalion, Royal Engineers, came with the South African War, fought over immense distances. Part of the Battalion was mobilised and dispatched to South Africa in September 1899, but it was soon besieged in Ladysmith with the army commanded by General Sir George White. However, further telegraph sections followed and the Royal Engineer Telegraph Service became responsible for constructing and operating telegraph command and administrative lines over an enormous area. The dividing point between the civil Post Office and the Royal Engineers for both telegraph and railway working was De Aar Junction on the main railway line. The instruments used for telegraphy were the morse operated sounder and the Wheatstone high-speed automatic equipment.[2] For field lines, cable was laid from a two-wheeled cable cart, but towards the end of the war a new type of cable wagon with a limber came into use; the prototype of a pattern that lasted until about 1937, when the horse disappeared from the Royal Corps of Signals. It is rather strange that no mechanical means of laying field cable has yet been devised that can equal, in accuracy and speed of laying, the cable wagon with its six-horse team and mounted linemen.

At Army Headquarters in South Africa there was both a Royal Engineer officer as Director of Telegraphs and an infantry officer as Director of Army Signalling. Each cavalry regiment, infantry battalion, and artillery battery had its visual signallers, and mounted signal companies were formed from them to provide visual communication from formation headquarters.

On 6 December 1899 heliograph communications were established between General White's force besieged in Ladysmith and the relieving column under General Sir Redvers Buller; and thereafter communications were maintained throughout the remainder of the siege except when the sun was obscured.

During the guerilla phase of the war the whole of the telegraph service in South Africa was put under the control of the Royal Engineer Director of Telegraphs, and was divided into four areas, each composed of districts under NCO inspectors. Operation was carried out as far as possible by the civil staffs and in the Boer Republics the telegraph offices were manned jointly by the RE Telegraph Service and re-engaged Boer civilians.[3]

There was a considerable development in signal organisation as a result of the Boer War. In 1907 seven divisional telegraph companies were formed, each of three sections with a cable wagon apiece. There were also three cable sections for the cavalry division, and telegraph companies of various natures for army and corps communications and the lines of communication. Visual signallers were included in the divisional companies and the cavalry cable sections, and telephones were added to equipment tables.[4]

In 1910 the term 'telegraph' was replaced by 'signal' in unit titles, and in the following year an Army Order announced the establishment of the Signal Service as part of the Corps of Royal Engineers.

In 1912 the cavalry division's signals were reorganised into a signal squadron, and a wireless signal company was formed for communication between army headquarters in the field and the cavalry division. The infantry divisional signal company was expanded to include a brigade signal section for each of the three infantry brigades, and similar provision was later made for brigade signal troops in the cavalry divisional signal squadron.

In the Army that mobilised in 1914 each major headquarters was provided with a signal squadron or company (which now included motor-cycle despatch riders) and there were additional airline and cable sections for allocation as necessary.[5] The two main means of communication were line telegraphy and despatch rider. Telephones were not in general use except in the rear areas and the artillery. Visual, under the conditions of trench warfare was hardly practicable, as it exposed the operator and gave away the locations of headquarters. Wireless communications were little used on the Western Front because of the lavish provision of lines. By the following year the advantages of the telephone had become so apparent that it was the normal method of communication, except for formal orders and reports, which were transmitted by telegraph.[6]

Telephones were not an unmixed blessing; for it was not at first realised by commanders and staff officers how vulnerable earth return circuits were to enemy interception, and much valuable information was given away by indiscreet conversations. To counter this, all concerned were alerted to the danger, earth return circuits were replaced where possible by metallic circuits, code names were allotted to formations and units, and signal officers were given call signs for telegraphic use.[7] In addition, the interception of telegraph circuits was made more difficult by the introduction of the fullerphone, invented by Captain (later Major-General) A. C. Fuller. This instrument transmitted a very small direct current, impossible to detect within a practicable range by the instruments then available to the Germans.[8]

Though wireless got off to a bad start on the Western Front, it was extensively used in the Mesopotamian campaign. There the 41st Wireless Company had .5kW Marconi pack sets, each complete equipment being carried on six pack horses. The scheduled range for these spark transmitters was 30 miles, but lower Mesopotamia is so flat that it was possible to work regularly over 100 miles. In autumn 1915 the Company, now designated No 1 Wireless Signal Squadron, got the much bigger 1.5kW Marconi sets, each carried in a special four-horse limbered wagon. With these, communication could be guaranteed over 150 miles, and under favourable conditions as much as 350 miles were worked. Using these sets communications were maintained with Kut throughout the siege.[9]

On the Western Front, in 1917, the British Field Wireless Set (or Trench Set, Spark, 50 Watts) was issued. As it was extremely simple to use, its popular title inevitably led to its being referred to as the 'BF Set'. To communicate with the divisional BF sets, there were at corps headquarters the more powerful Wilson spark transmitters, with effective ranges of 4-10 miles.[10] In the same year the first continuous wave wireless sets were tried, and their success led to an order for 822 — primarily for use between artillery batteries and observation posts. Later they were used for tank brigade communications.[11] During the German spring offensive of 1918 wireless was frequently the only means of communication, for the complex line system of deep buried multi-core cables was overrun by the enemy's rapid advance.[12]

After the war, and in the light of its lessons, it was decided that the Signal Service of the Royal Engineers should be replaced by a separate Corps of Signals. The formation of this was approved by Royal Warrant on 2 July 1920, and on 5 August the King conferred the title of Royal. For a large number of the officers and most of the other ranks, the transition from RE Signal Service to Royal Corps of Signals merely entailed a change of cap badge, and the traditions of the former were inherited by the latter. Even the badge, the figure of Mercury, was not new, for it had been adopted as the insignia of the Telegraph Battalion RE, soon after its formation in 1884, at the suggestion of Captain (later Colonel) C. F. C. Beresford, whose father had purchased a statue of Mercury at the Great Exhibition of 1851.[13]

At the end of the war two new types of continuous wave wireless sets had been coming into production, the 120W and the 500W with respective ranges of 30 and 300 miles, and they remained in use for many years. They were to be followed by a series designated by letters, according to range, but only the A set, a portable ground set for infantry brigades with a range of six miles, and the C set for infantry divisions, with a 20-mile range, ever materialised. The C set was either carried in a one-ton truck, or, as the C Set Indian Pack, on pack mules. For armoured fighting vehicles there were three types of radio telephone set; one for regimental headquarters and two for mounting in AFVs with the far too short respective ranges of five and two miles. By 1929 a new series of sets, designated by numbers, had been formulated. Three of these were for use in the field — the No 1 for infantry and artillery brigades, and No 2 for divisions, and the No 3 for corps. All of them included radio telephony.

In 1928 the General Post Office took a decision which had important effects on the Royal Signals; the replacement of morse sounders by the new teleprinter equipment. This deprived the Corps of a potential reserve of trained morse operators, and in 1933, therefore, sounders were replaced by teleprinters for all army communications in rear of corps headquarters. From corps headquarters forward the morse fullerphone was retained.[14]

As a separate arm of the service, the Royal Corps of Signals had its first major test in the field during the short campaign of 1940 in France and Flanders. It was an exacting test because there was a shortage of Regular signal units. GHQ Signals was a Supplementary Reserve unit, whilst the signals for the II Corps and the 4th Division came from the Territorial Army — the former being the London Corps Signals and the latter the 54th East Anglian Divisional Signals. The London Corps Signals moved to France in September 1939 without any post-mobilisation training, and only the prewar enthusiasm of its personnel, many of whom gave up their winter week ends to take technical courses, enabled the unit to provide communications for the II Corps.

On 10 May 1940 the Germans attacked in the West, and in accordance with prearranged plans, the British and French forces of the Allied left wing swung forward into Belgium and southern Holland. The II Corps advanced on a one-divisional front. The 3rd Division led, followed by the 4th Division, whilst the 50th Division was behind in reserve. Control of the movement was exercised by five route regulation posts, placed at intervals along the route between the Belgian frontier and Brussels. These were linked to each other and to a route regulation centre by Belgian telephone lines and by wireless. The former could only be arranged after the troops crossed the frontier, and how far the Belgians would help was unknown. A special party to liaise with the Belgian Posts and Telegraphs and the wireless sets for the route regulation posts were provided by the II Corps Signals, who also had to connect Headquarters II Corps by field cable to the nearest route

regulation post. The other tasks that the unit had to undertake were to provide the parties to open the new signal offices and signal centres required for the moves of the Corps headquarters, to operate the existing Corps signal offices, and to hand over existing communications to GHQ Signals after Headquarters II Corps moved.

II Corps Signals had two wireless sections, each of four No 3 sets. These worked well and were very reliable. One of their advantages was that they could work satisfactorily with their roof aerials when concealed inside barns — and Flanders abounds in barns. A major disadvantage in wireless communications was that the BEF was over-sensitive to enemy direction finding; wireless sets were not allowed within 2,000 yards of Corps Headquarters, nor could they be in front of it or behind it as one looked towards the enemy. The sets were accordingly grouped in two localities, known as radio villages, north and south of Corps Headquarters and connected to the signal office by line. From each radio village 'control' an omnibus circuit went round all the sets in the group.

The advance into Belgium went reasonably smoothly and communications, in spite of unexpected difficulties, worked well. The subsequent problems experienced by signals during this short campaign may perhaps best be shown by quotations from reminiscences by the author, who had been the Regular adjutant of the unit before the war and who was then commanding No 2 Company:

'14 May. I went forward early to Brussels to take over the new signal office. A girls' school had been requisitioned for HQ II Corps. We had very ample, clean, and airy cellar accommodation for the signal office and an office upstairs for the unit Command Group.

'15 May. Our circuit record showed a very presentable list of communications and the wireless groups were in their new sites. All lines were working, though we had had trouble with those to 3rd Division being cut by shell fire during the night. Maintenance parties had had a difficult job in the dark in an unknown area. At about midday we were told to put two pairs of the International Cable through from Brussels to the civil exchange at Denderleeuw (about 12 miles west of Brussels), and to extend them another six miles further west by quad cable to a point south of Vondelen. This was "in case of withdrawal".

'16 May. At 0400 hours I was aroused and ordered to a conference at the signal office immediately. The BEF was withdrawing. The unit Advanced Group moved off in the morning to establish the new signal office at Vondelen. The Rear Group moved in the afternoon. Congestion on the roads was appalling. I passed a column of 3rd Division transport standing nose to tail for miles along a narrow pavé road without any cover. The Vondelen signal office was in a small farm. The road congestion affected us badly. The line sections with the Advanced Group had already run out of cable. I sent an officer back to bring up some more, but although he could get through the mass of vehicles on a motor cycle, he could not get cable lorries back to the signal office, though several routes were tried. The situation was saved by the arrival of two cable detachments of the Rear Group from a northerly direction, who had missed their way to the billeting area.

'17 May. By midday we had line communications to everybody concerned. HQ 3rd and 4th Divisions had just withdrawn to the line of the River Dendre, but the staff did not know where they were and we had to send out reconnaissance officers ahead of our laying cable detachments to look for them. The demand on despatch riders was now extremely heavy and we had reliefs of 20 to 25 at a time, which was more than our resources could stand for long. One of our cable detachments was captured, but escaped again under a stout-hearted NCO. A line section, cheerfully reeling in cable in a village which had been vacated by our troops and apparently had Germans on three sides of it, was rescued in the nick of time.

'18 May. After a long night move of 50 miles without lights, Rear Group arrived at Wambréchies, north of Lille, and set up a new signal office for Corps Headquarters in the basement of a large chateau. One of our old routes gave us good lateral communications to III Corps at Roncq, to the north.

'19 May. In the afternoon I went out to see 1st Divisional Signals, as 1st Division had just come under command of II Corps, and we were building a line to them. It was this visit which brought home to me the importance of signal officers keeping themselves up to date with the operational situation by frequent visits to the Intelligence staff. I found Lieutenant-Colonel Nalder in conference with a worried divisional staff, who had heard rumour of a German penetration at Douai towards their right rear, whilst their own brigades were still retiring along the roads in front. I was able to reassure them by producing a rough copy of the Corps situation map.

'*20 May*. German penetration to the south was becoming much more pronounced and the situation was changing so rapidly that we were unable to keep our location list up to date. Despatch riders sent out to Ordnance and RASC units were unable to reach their destinations as the Germans were ahead of them. Capture of the packets they carried might, of course, have had serious results, and we started drawing a red boundary on our location maps beyond which DRs were not allowed to go without special authority.

'*21 May*. The Wambréchies signal office was now a successful concern, but in the afternoon we were ordered to move to Armentières.

'*22 May*. The move to Armentières was completed smoothly, but the signal office was rather cramped, occupying a space cleared in the enormous cellars of a wine warehouse. (The signalmaster found himself in the peculiar position of issuing wines and spirits on indent from staff messes!)

'*23 May*. At this time all three headquarters were close together. I and II Corps were both in Armentières and III Corps was at Ploegstreet, about four miles to the north. GHQ was at Premesques, and nearer to the headquarters of some of the divisions than were the corps headquarters. HQ II Corps announced another move; this time to Quesnoy, four miles north of Wambréchies, and the unit Advanced Group moved off to establish a signal office there.

'*24 May*. Armentières was bombed heavily, and the signal office had several near misses. The Corps Headquarters site was entirely surrounded by canals, which from an anti-tank point of view was ideal, but the bridges over the canals must have been tempting targets. Some of our lines were cut, chiefly by falling buildings. They included the lateral to HQ I Corps, which is so far unique in signal history, as it was only half a mile long and was built by a line maintenance section. Bombing started again about 1800; more lines were cut and line maintenance detachments had a busy time. The move to Quesnoy was postponed.

'*25 May*. Three more heavy raids this morning. It was becoming increasingly difficult to keep communications through. It was decided, therefore, to move Corps Headquarters to Lomme, on the western outskirts of Lille. Advanced Group was ordered to establish a signal office there and dismantle the one at Quesnoy. Corps Headquarters moved in the evening. Construction of lines in the time available had not been easy, as we now had 1st, 3rd, 4th and 5th Divisions in II Corps. Communications were through to the first three at a late hour of the night, but the line to 5th Division was not through till about 1000 hours on the following day. The line went through Armentières, which was now a blazing ruin, and it was cut at a number of places in the town. Eventually we sent a second detachment to build a by-pass east of Armentières.

'Wireless communications were always through during these operations and our No 3 sets handled a great quantity of traffic; but the greatest demand from our staff was always for speech channels.'

On 26 May the withdrawal to the coast began in earnest and the bulk of

II Corps Signals was ordered to move there, leaving the wireless sections and despatch riders to maintain skeleton communications.

As a result of this campaign better provision was made for mobile operations. Armoured command vehicles were designed for armoured divisions and five of these carried main divisional headquarters. An ACV was divided into two compartments, the rear one for the staff and the front one for the wireless operators and their sets. A different wireless net was operated from each vehicle (divisional command radio telephony, administrative, artillery, rear link, etc), and short range wireless connected all vehicles. The success of this scheme led to similar non-armoured command vehicles being built for corps and infantry divisional headquarters. All these were Royal Signals vehicles.

For long distance communications in all theatres of war, much reliance was placed on permanent line, and Royal Signals brought standards of communication which had never been known before in some countries. In Persia, for instance, trunk lines were composed of single strands of galvanised iron wire, slung to poles with frequently defective insulators. They were not terminated on exchanges, and telephone conversations had to be arranged by telegraph beforehand. However, even then the line was often too bad for speech to be audible. Over the lines constructed and maintained by the Royal Signals and the Indian Signal Corps it was possible to talk from Baghdad to Tehran or Cairo, and from Tehran to Abadan with a clarity and strength equal to that expected over Post Office trunk circuits in the United Kingdom. This was achieved by high quality construction with copper wire and by using multi-channel carrier equipment with repeaters installed about every hundred miles.

Wireless equipment made enormous strides during the war, primarily due to the need for speech during mobile operations over much longer ranges than had been envisaged. Without first class wireless communications the handling of an armoured division in battle, for instance, would have been impossible. Subsequently the advance in wireless (or radio, as it is now customarily called) techniques has led to its replacing line almost entirely on the battlefield.

It is well known by the Royal Corps of Signals that communications are never noticed till they fail, and all signal officers would agree with St Paul that 'Evil communications corrupt good manners.'[15]

Below: **1st Division Telegraph Battalion Royal Engineers, on parade with band and GS wagons, on Salisbury Plain in 1886.** / *RHQ Royal Signals*

Top right: **A cable detachment of the Royal Engineers Signal Service in 1890.** / *RHQ Royal Signals*

Centre right: **The Telegraph Operating Room at Johannesburg in the Boer War. Operators of the Royal Engineers using telegraph sounder instruments.** / *RHQ Royal Signals*

Below right: **An RE Signal Service cable section on manoeuvres, 1910.** / *RHQ Royal Signals*

Above left: F Cable Section crossing the River Marne during the advance at the battle of the Marne in 1914. / *RHQ Royal Signals*

Left: A cable detachment RE Signals in Italy during World War I. / *RHQ Royal Signals*

Above: Advanced Headquarters I Corps and Headquarters 7th Division at the battle of Tikrit, north of Baghdad, 5-6 November 1917. (The signalman on the right is transmitting by heliograph to a formation — probably a brigade — to the right of the picture, whilst his companion is reading the replies through a telescope). / *RHQ Royal Signals*

Right: 'Through'. Reproduction of a famous painting by the late Sergeant Franc P. Martin, RE Signal Service, depicting a lineman, killed after repairing a telephone cable on the Western Front during World War I. / *RHQ Royal Signals*

Left: An operator of the Royal Signals with a No 1 wireless set, mounted on an elephant and providing communications for the police during the Hindu festival at Hardwar on the Ganges in 1938. / *RHQ Royal Signals*

Below left: A divisional headquarters command vehicle, Royal Signals, in the Western Desert, 1941. / *RHQ Royal Signals*

Right: A Royal Signals line patrol under fire at Anzio, 1943. / *RHQ Royal Signals*

Below: A wireless detachment of the 6th Airborne Division at the Rhine crossing in 1945. Note Royal Signals operator wearing the Divisional flash. / *RHQ Royal Signals*

6

Supply and Transport

Whatever views may be held as to his ability to command in the field, there can be no doubt that Sir Redvers Buller was very competent and far-sighted as a Quartermaster-General; and during his tenure of that office, his appreciation of the importance of the Army's logistical support resulted in the formation in 1888 of the Army Service Corps.

Before 1869 the functions of supply and transport had been the separate responsibilities of various corps and organisations with different designations. In that year the two functions had been linked under clumsy titles indicating the two activities. The Corps which emerged in 1888, however, was something entirely different; for it was a combatant regiment with terms of service for officers and other ranks which were similar to those of the rest of the Army.

After its formation, the Army Service Corps had some experience of active service in such minor campaigns as those in the Gambia, Ashanti, and the Sudan, before facing its first real test in the South African War of 1899-1902. Soon after the outbreak of the war, transport units as well as reinforcements of individual officers and men were sent out to South Africa, coming under the command of the creator of the Corps, Sir Redvers Buller. Rather strangely, in view of his appreciation of the unity of the two functions, Buller, before handing over the chief command to Lord Roberts, appointed separate Directors of Supply and Transport, on the grounds that responsibility for both was too heavy a charge for one man.

Army Service Corps Companies, equipped mainly with mule or ox-drawn vehicles, provided first and second line transport for units, as well as supply and ammunition columns. All transport could be concentrated when required under the senior transport officer on the spot.

The transport companies had British officers, NCOs, and artificers, but the drivers were civilians ('Cape boys'). In a mule company there were 130 drivers, 520 mules, and 50 vehicles; whilst an ox company had 200 drivers, 1,600 oxen, and 100 wagons.

Transport was never sufficient to meet all the Army's needs, and after Lord Roberts arrived as Commander-in-Chief, his Chief of Staff, Sir Herbert Kitchener, obtained his approval to concentrating all except first line vehicles into a common stock. It did not result in any improvement, and first line transport suffered from the withdrawal of close ASC help and experience. Buller, who still commanded in Natal, retained the earlier, and now well understood, organisation; and records show that his transport functioned better and with less wastage of animals than did that, as organised by Kitchener, under Roberts' immediate command. As a result there was, throughout the theatre of operations, a gradual reversion to the old system.

A small amount of steam road transport was operated by the Royal Engineers, but it did not make any major contribution to operations.

As a result of the many lessons learned during the South African War, the Army Service Corps devised an organisation to meet the Army's needs for a war in Europe. Space does not allow an explanation of the changes involved, but they enabled the Army Service Corps to deal with the massive supply problems of World War I. A major factor, however, in the movement of supplies was the advent of mechanical vehicles. Without these it is doubtful whether the roads in rear could have

accommodated the transport columns; for there would have been such a vast number of slow moving horse-drawn wagons.

The basic ASC problem was firstly to organise the two sorts of transport — horse and mechanical — in relation to the resources in animals and the reserves of suitable mechanical vehicles in civilian hands throughout the country, and secondly to establish a system of provisioning food and forage which would be immune to any interference from food hoarding and famine prices.

About 900 mechanical vehicles were held for the original Expeditionary Force, and there was a subsidy system operating in peace to provide for expansion in war. But the needs of the vastly bigger Army had to be met by impressment, as well as by manufacture at home and abroad.

To ensure that food and forage were immediately available for shipping overseas on the outbreak of war, contracts were prepared in peace for commodities to be despatched to depots in the United Kingdom, established on general mobilisation.

The Army Service Corps of 1914 was organised in combined supply and transport horsed divisional trains for each division, and other trains for non-divisional units. Transport behind the second line was almost entirely mechanised, with solid tyred 3ton lorries, and organised into various types of units, such as divisional supply columns, ammunition columns, and companies for general use. Within the division the ASC provided all the artillery transport requirements, including gun tractors. Petrol, food, and forage were held at depots located at bases and on the lines of communication. This basic organisation was common to all theatres of war. In Europe it was little altered during the course of the war, but elsewhere there were considerable modifications to meet conditions of climate and terrain. Pack animals of all kinds had in places to be substituted for horse drawn vehicles, and light vans for 3 ton lorries.

Before the war the strength of the ASC had been about 500 officers and 6,000 men. By the end of it there were some 320,000 all ranks; but the number of men who served in the ASC was far greater, for casualties were heavy and about 80,000 were transferred to the infantry during the course of the war. In December 1918 the Army Service Corps was responsible for about 165,000 vehicles, including motorcycles. In that same month the designation 'Royal' was added to the title of the Corps in recognition of its distinguished services.

In the drastic reduction of the Army's strength at the conclusion of the war, the Royal Army Service Corps suffered more than most arms of the Service. Its strength was reduced below that even required to support the small peacetime Army on the grounds that, as the general nature of RASC duties in war were comparable to those of equivalent civilian agencies, men would be readily available to bring units up to war establishment. This argument had been proved false before, and it resulted in the Corps being so under strength that realistic training was practically impossible; particularly as the Treasury would not allow transport to be used on exercises if it entailed hiring civilian vehicles to carry out normal routine garrison duties.

The training of officers inevitably suffered from the lack of practical training in their units, and the courses run for them in the Training Centre did little to prepare them for their duties in war. However, there was a considerable improvement in the 1930s, which owed much to the allocation of RASC units to the formations with which they would operate in the field, combined with the transfer of responsibility for the training and manning of the RASC from the Quartermaster-General to the General Staff and the Adjutant-General, thus placing the Corps on the same footing as the other combatant arms. The reorganisation was accompanied by a more forward look in the Training Centre and by some relaxation in financial restrictions.

A major development after World War I was the elimination of the horse from second line transport. Although the majority of the Army's third line transport was mechanical by the end of the war, the essential second line had remained horsed. It was now reorganised on a mechanical basis, and the RASC virtually ceased to be a mounted arm of the Service. The carriage of ammunition in the second line, previously the responsibility of the Royal Artillery horsed divisional ammunition column, was now transferred to the RASC. Forage, a bulky load for all echelons, still had to be carried for horsed first line transport and for mounted units not yet mechanised.

The establishment of a small Supplementary Reserve of officers, and the granting of some short service commissions did something to ease the shortage of officers, but, nevertheless, the start of World War II found that Corps still seriously short of officers and men.

A problem facing the Army between the two great wars had been the design and production of a suitable general transport vehicle with some cross-country performance — a quality that the solid tyred vehicles of World War I did not possess. Tracked vehicles were being developed, but they had obvious disadvantages on roads. The RASC was charged with responsibility for the development of wheeled vehicles for the Army. Six-wheeled vehicles were designed and produced which, together with very satisfactory four-wheeled vehicles with large low pressure tyres, met a large proportion of RASC requirements of mobilisation. It had been hoped before the war that these designs would be adopted for general commercial use through a subsidy scheme. Mainly for financial reasons this idea was not a success. The vehicles remained a standard army type, but owing to the very large needs of the now mechanised army, recourse had to be made to impressment of civilian vehicles, previously earmarked in peace. These were used to complete the Expeditionary Force to establishment, and immediate steps had to be taken, in addition, to obtain vehicles in the hands of manufacturers. Owing to the vast increase in mechanical transport, responsibility for the provision of wheeled vehicles was removed from the RASC.

Throughout the war the ever increasing demand for vehicles was met by manufacturers both at home and in North America. Many of these had four-wheel drive, which was needed particularly for traversing deserts. American 10 ton lorries were used a great deal for load carrying, where they were suitable, but the backbone of maintenance transport throughout the war was the 3 ton lorry.

There were occasions when the available transport was insufficient to meet all the operational needs. In Libya in 1940-41, for instance, the main reason for the inability of the Western Desert force to advance beyond the Cyrenaica/Tripolitania frontier was the lack of transport to maintain it; again, the advance after the rapidly retreating enemy in North-West Europe in 1944 was hampered by the lack of transport, particularly for petrol.

For special loads, such as tanks, Royal Engineer bridging material, and other heavy equipment, special vehicles were produced and were operated in formed units in considerable numbers.

There had been an improvement in the peacetime standard of messing in the Army and for war the field service ration was redesigned to include a range of tinned or preserved foods to replace the 'hard fare' which had previously been issued when fresh food could not be distributed. Adequate planning between the War Office and the Ministry of Food ensured a ration to meet the needs of the armies in the field. In general the required standard was maintained throughout the war in all theatres, subject to difficulties over shipping or local supply; and it is probable that no army was ever better fed in wartime.

In World War I the provision and transport of petrol, oil, and lubricants had not been a main problem, because requirements were normally in the rear echelons and could be handled through supply channels. The advent of the completely mechanised army, however, presented a very different picture, and one which was the subject of considerable study. The pump system of petrol supply was obviously impracticable in a mobile war, and bulk tankers were not available in quantity, even if they had been suitable for detail issue. It was therefore decided to use cans; for the four-gallon can was in widespread use throughout the world, was easily handled, and could be manufactured fairly rapidly. However, it had not been realised how easily the four-gallon can could be broken in transport. Though the cans were packed two to a case, losses were suffered, even in military railway wagons and lorries travelling along roads. Once the latter left the road losses could amount to 50%.

The German petrol containers captured in the Western Desert were so much better than the four-gallon cans that Headquarters Middle-East requested a similar pattern. Construction of these was put in hand immediately, and by the end of the war some 50 million had been produced. They were known as 'jerricans' after the British soldier's name of Jerry for his German opponent.

Most cans were filled in the vicinity of ports, though, later, pipe lines were used, including one across the Channel (PLUTO). But operations in North-West Europe were hampered in the early stages by a lack of capacity to convey petroleum products from the ports to the consumers, including the Royal Air Force.

Supply and transport in World War II covered, not only carriage on land, but also on the sea and in the air. Supply by air, including both dropping and landing all the items required by troops in action, was developed in the Burma campaign, and by 1945 most supplies in that theatre were being delivered by air. At sea the Royal Army Service Corps eventually operated a large number of vessels, including schooners in the Mediterranean, and load carrying amphibians called DUKWs (from the American maker's code, and pronounced 'ducks') in landing operations.

Buller's amalgamation of supply and transport into one Corps had worked well under war conditions, but transport was always the dominating function. In World War I barely one tenth of the Army Service Corps was engaged in supply duties. But the apparent ease with which these duties had been performed, coupled with the reduction of the responsibilities for supply in peace, had the unfortunate result that supply personnel were so reduced in numbers as to be quite inadequate to supply cadres for training and for expansion in war. The difficulties were, in fact, overcome, nevertheless it was increasingly questioned as to whether supply and transport were indivisible. The carriage of food and forage had once been the Army's predominant requirement of its road transport, but in World War II food represented only about 10% of loads carried. It was therefore not logical to require a predominantly transport corps to be responsible for the provision of food if the responsibility for the provision of ammunition and other warlike stores was allocated elsewhere. (Petrol, oil and lubricants, were in a rather different category, because the RASC, in addition to providing them, was a major user.)

About five years after the end of the war a committee was assembled to consider the allocation of duties amongst the administrative services. No immediate action was taken on their recommendations, but some ten years later another committee made similar recommendations, and these were accepted. The result was that responsibility for the provision of both food and petrol etc was transferred from the Royal Army Service Corps to the Royal Army Ordnance Corps. At the same time, the operation of railways, inland waterways, and docks was transferred from the Royal Engineers to the Royal Army Service Corps, which was renamed the Royal Corps of Transport in 1965.

Thus, after 85 years the supply and transport arrangements of the British Army have come to conform generally with those of most of the major foreign armies.

7

Stores and Repair

'There is probably no branch of the Army which has seen greater changes or passed through greater vicissitudes than the Ordnance Stores Department. With an antiquity which passes beyond the limits of recorded history, its existence has been so interwoven with the other Services that it is a matter of no small difficulty to disentangle the threads and present a clear sketch of its history. At one time civilian, at another military, now associated with the Artillery, now with the Engineers, it carries us back a long way into the remote history of the British Forces, covering a period of nearly five hundred years. The first official entry which discloses the existence of an Ordnance Department in England is in 1418, when John Louth appears to have been "Clerk of the Ordnance".'

So wrote A. M. Chichester and G. Burges-Short in their great history of the regiments and corps of the British Army.[1]

After the Crimean War the old Board of Ordnance was swept away and replaced by a Military Stores Department, and in 1865 an establishment of soldiers was authorised under the title of Military Store Staff Corps. In 1869 the Military Store Department and the Military Staff Corps, together with the other 'Departments' of the Army, (Commissariat, Transport, Purveyors, Barracks, and Pay), were absorbed into the Control Department. This broke up in 1875, and in 1881 the companies performing Ordnance Store duties were designated Ordnance Store Corps, and, with the Military Store Department, they came under the Director of Artillery. Before the end of the century they were joined to become the Army Ordnance Department, and the ordnance officer's responsibilities for the stores in his charge and as an adviser to his commander on the supply of war material were laid down.[2]

With World War I came the problem of recovery and repair of armoured fighting vehicles. The Tank Corps had its own workshops when it was first formed, and in 1917 tank salvage companies were created to recover tanks immobilised on the battlefield. The organisation for recovery and repair soon became so efficient that the then Colonel J. F. C. Fuller was able to comment of the battle of Cambrai in 1917: 'It was a remarkable feat that at 8am on 30 November not one machine of 2 Brigade was fit for action, yet by 6am on 1 December no fewer than 73 tanks had been launched against the enemy with decisive effect.'[3]

After World War I the immense achievement in the supply of war material and munitions to the Army in the field was recognised by the renaming of the Army Ordnance Department as the Royal Army Ordnance Corps.[4]

In 1920 an officer organisation was introduced into the RAOC which was unique in the Army. Officers were divided into three categories. The first of these was composed of 'Directing Staff Officers', who were designated both by class and by rank. An Ordnance Officer 1st Class, for instance, was a colonel or above, whilst one of the 4th Class was a captain. Officers in this category had transferred to the RAOC after some years' service in other branches of the Army and they had therefore a broad experience of the needs and functions of various arms of the Service. They filled all the higher posts in the RAOC and the Ordnance staff appointments on the static and field headquarters. They also held the commands of stores and ammunition depots. The second category was the Workshop Branch; the officers belonging to which were styled Inspectors of Ordnance Machinery (IOM), and an IOM 1st Class was a lieutenant-colonel. In 1924 the title was changed to Ordnance Mechanical Engineer (OME). The third category consisted of officers who had been commissioned from warrant rank as Ordnance Executive Officers, and workshop officers who had been commissioned from other ranks in the Armourer Section as Assistant Inspectors of Armourers.[5]

There were three branches of other rank tradesmen: Store, Armament Artificer, and Armourer. The Store Branch consisted of clerks, storemen, and artisans. Ranks unique to the RAOC were those of conductor and sub-conductor, both warrant officers Class I of the Store Branch. Together with master gunners 1st class and staff sergeant-majors 1st class, they were senior to all other WOs Class I in the Army.[6]

All technical ammunition matters came under the Chief Inspector of Armaments (CIA), and there were a number of Inspecting Ordnance Officers at home and overseas, whose duties included the inspection, proof, sentencing, and minor repair of ammunition.[7]

In 1927 the responsibility for all wheeled mechanical transport, except that of the RASC and RAMC, was transferred from the Quartermaster-General to the Master-General of the Ordnance. The RAOC was similarly moved and took over the duties of the receipt, storage, issue, and repair of MGO vehicles.[8]

In 1933 the RAOC lost one of its activities with the closure of the Royal Army Clothing Department, though the Corps still remained responsible for the patterns, storage, and issue of army clothing.[9]

Four years later the appointment of Master-General of the Ordnance was discontinued. The MGO Department was merged with that of the Director-General of Munitions Production and the RAOC returned again to the responsibility of the Quartermaster-General.[10]

These various reorganisations did not affect the basic task of the RAOC, which was to ensure that stores reached the troops in the quantity and at the time required, and in a condition fit for use.[11]

Little was done in the years between the two world wars to implement the lessons learned in recovering tanks, and no armoured recovery vehicles were built. Organisations and equipment tried out in the 1920s disappeared in the 1930s; casualties of the cuts in Service expenditure. Responsibility for mechanical engineering had got hopelessly confused; so much so that when the half-track lorry was introduced, the RAOC was responsible for the repair and provision of spare parts for the rear or tracked half, whilst the RASC was responsible for the front or wheeled half![12]

When war broke out in 1939 the RAOC consisted of two main branches, stores and workshops, and these two branches were reflected in staff appointments. At GHQ British Expeditionary Force there was a Director of Ordnance Stores (DOS) and a Principal Officer Mechanical Engineering (POME). At corps headquarters the appointments were Assistant Director of Ordnance Stores (ADOS) and Chief Officer Mechanical Engineering (COME), whilst divisional HQ had a Deputy Assistant Director of Ordnance Stores (DADOS) and a Senior Officer Mechanical Engineering (SOME). Each corps had an ordnance field park in which was a section for each division, one for corps troops, and one in reserve. Of army field workshops, there was one in each division, one for GHQ troops, and one for the anti-aircraft brigade. Other RAOC units included base ordnance depots, base ammunition depots, a base ordnance workshop, and a port workshop detachment.[13] All the above, however, were either Territorial Army or scratch units, for no Regular field force Ordnance units existed.[14] The organisation of the GHQ Troops Workshop is of some interest. Its main workshop served units in the GHQ area; but there was also a Main Recovery Section with the primary task of light recovery (principally for artillery) but which could also act as a workshop. In addition there were six line of communications recovery sections, for heavy recovery between the army field workshops and railhead.[15]

The RAOC had to deal with a number of special problems during the early campaigns in the Western Desert. Owing to the limited amount of transport in the Sidi Barrani operations, Field Supply Depots had to be established well forward, containing ammunition, water, petrol, and supplies. A great deal of special construction and modification had to be undertaken to meet special requirements of desert warfare, notably work on 161 tanks which, on arrival from the United Kingdom, had to be modified in the Base Workshops before they were suitable for desert conditions. There were no vehicles capable of recovering infantry tanks in the desert and civilian vehicles had to be purchased and fitted with winches, cranes and other equipment. Distilled water had to be produced and containers made for it, and the RAOC filled anti-tank mines which both they and the Royal Engineers manufactured.[16]

Due to the lack of suitable British equipment, German superiority in tank recovery during the early North African battles was marked. For instance, in the summer of 1941 in Operation Battleaxe it was claimed that over 100 enemy tanks had been knocked out, but the Germans retained possession of the battlefield and were able to salvage all but 12[17]. British organisation, however, improved rapidly, and during the second battle of El Alamein over 1,000 tanks belonging to X Corps alone were repaired in workshops and returned to battle within three weeks.[18]

As the RE Signal Service eventually developed into the Royal Corps of Signals, so it became apparent that the repair and recovery side of the RAOC was becoming a specialist branch of its own, and its formation into the independent Corps of Royal Electrical and Mechanical Engineers was authorised by Army Order 70 of May 1942. Repair and recovery of equipment and vehicles lay in the province of the new corps, whilst the RAOC remained responsible for the provision, storage, and supply of all ordnance stores, vehicles and ammunition, and for the repair of ammunition, clothing and general stores. All RAOC workshop units were transferred to REME and the reorganisation was completed by 1 October 1942. In connection with the new organisation, the RASC ceased to supply and repair its own vehicles; the former responsibility, together with vehicles and MT stores holding units, being transferred to the RAOC, and the latter to REME.[19]

The first British armoured recovery vehicles were based on various types of tank and used to support armoured regiments equipped with those tanks, but they did not have winches. The best British armoured recovery vehicle was the Churchill ARV Mark II, incorporating the chassis of the Churchill tanks Marks III and IV, and this had a winch, with a pull of 25 tons. It also had a fixed rear jib with a lift of 15 ton and a dismountable forward jib with a lift of $7\frac{1}{2}$ ton. It did not appear, however, until late in 1944.[20]

To emphasise again the vital importance of recovery, an American estimate was that 60% of battle casualties were repairable. In 21 Army Group it was reckoned that these battle casualties accounted for about 30% of the tasks undertaken in AFV workshops, the remaining 70% being made up of repairs to mechanical faults, modifications, and faults due to lack of maintenance. One division lost 48 Sherman tanks on a minefield. REME recovered and repaired these, returning 32 of them to the division within 48 hours.[21]

Weapons and Equipment

8
Weapons

The years following World War II have seen a greater change in the weapons of the Army than has any similar period of its history. The primary reason for this is the enormous advance in the science of electronics and the consequent advent of the guided missile. A secondary reason lies in the need to counter the formidable main battle tanks and their attendant swarms of light armoured fighting vehicles.

Small Arms
In the 1950s the British Army bade farewell to the bolt-action rifle that had served it so well for over half a century. The replacement was a self-loading rifle produced by the Belgian Fabrique National d'Armes de Guerre (or FN), using the agreed standard NATO 7.62mm ammunition, and known as the Fusil Automatique Léger, or FAL. The United Kingdom was one of the many countries that adopted this FN FAL rifle, and a British version was manufactured. At about the same time the officer's revolver which, first as the Webley and then as the Enfield variation of it, had been used as long as the bolt-action rifle, was replaced by the Belgian Browning automatic pistol of 1935 pattern.

There was, too, a new machine gun, also a Belgian weapon, the FN Mitrailleur à Gaz (or MAG), taking the same standard 7.62mm ammunition and replacing both the Bren and Vickers guns. It is manufactured, with some modifications, by the Royal Small arms Factory at Enfield Lock as the General Purpose Machine Gun (GPMG).[1] In its light machine gun role it has not been particularly popular on account of its size and weight, but as a support gun on a tripod mounting and as a vehicle coaxial gun it is a satisfactory weapon.[2]

At the time of writing trials are being conducted by NATO to determine suitable replacements for existing self-loading rifles and light machine guns. The United Kingdom has submitted two entries called, respectively, the Individual Weapon (a combination of rifle and sub-machine gun) and the Light Support Weapon (a light machine gun). The two are basically the same, except that the latter has a heavier and larger barrel, a light bipod, and one or two other minor differences to enable it to fire automatically for prolonged periods. The intention is to equip an infantry section with a family of two weapons having a common ammunition, which will give much improved mobility and flexibility together with a better chance of hitting a target, using either single shot or automatic fire, at the ranges likely in future action. The respective weights to the two weapons are only $8\frac{1}{2}$lb and $10\frac{1}{2}$lb; but perhaps the most remarkable feature is the very small bore of 4.85mm or .191in, that is, even smaller than that of the .22in miniature range competition rifle; but the muzzle velocity is of course very much greater. The ammunition has been specially developed and is said to be capable of penetrating a steel helmet at over 500m; in addition, its light weight and size would enable an infantryman to carry a very large number of rounds. The magazine of the Individual Weapon holds 20 rounds and that of the Light Support Weapon 30 rounds, but the two are interchangeable. Both can fire in either single shot or automatic mode, and the recoil with both is slight. Both weapons have optical sights with x4 magnification.[3]

Mortars
There are two modern types of mortar. In the 1950s the Royal Armament Research and Development Establishment (RARDE) developed the 81mm mortar to replace the old 3in. It is a very accurate weapon and has a range of 4,500m with its standard charges 1 to 6, and 5,600m with charges 7 and 8. The rate of fire, which can be kept up indefinitely, is 15 rounds per minute, and because of its exceptional range it can often carry out tasks which would otherwise demand the use of field artillery. There is a special mounting for it to be fired from an armoured personnel carrier.[4]

A much lighter weapon is the new British 51mm mortar, which replaces the 2in mortar in the infantry platoon and which can be carried by one man on a sling. It can bring down quick and accurate fire on a platoon front and provide local smoke screens and target illumination for direct fire weapons out to the normal fighting range of the infantry's anti-tank recoilless guns. The maximum range for indirect fire is 800m, about double that of the 2in, and the minimum 150m. With direct fire the point blank minimum range is determined by the arming time of the fuse. The whole equipment weighs only 4.7kg including the monopod and sight, and six rounds fit into a webbing satchel which can be carried by hand or strapped on the back.[5]

Recoilless Guns
There are two categories of recoilless guns, a heavy and a light. The earlier of the heavy types was the Mobat 120mm with a range of about 820m. It can be towed on its two-wheeled trailer over rough country and is fired from it. A 7.62mm Bren light machine gun is mounted on the left side of the barrel.[6] Its successor is the 120mm Wombat, which is a good deal lighter than the Mobat and has a greater range. It is designed to be transported by and fired from either its two-wheeled trailer or an armoured personnel carrier. It has an optical battle sight which enables moving targets to be engaged up to 1,000m and stationary targets up to 1,450m. It fires high explosive squash head ammunition (for which see below) at a rate of four rounds per minute.[7]

The lighter recoilless gun is the 84mm Carl Gustav, designed in Sweden and bringing its name from its country of origin. It is a shoulder-controlled weapon, capable of destroying a tank at 400m. It weighs 36lb and can be carried and operated by one man; though a second man is needed as loader and ammunition carrier. The latter also carries the spare parts, and scouts ahead as a tank-hunter, if so required. The back blast, common to all these recoilless guns, gives a danger area of some 30m behind the gun, which has to be kept clear of all men and equipment. It fires a high explosive anti-tank shell (HEAT), stabilised by fins which open when it leaves the barrel and with a rocket motor to increase its speed. The motor comes into operation when the shell is about 18in from the muzzle and burns for one and a half seconds.[8]

Guns and Howitzers
Conventional ordnance and guided missile systems are complementary, rather than competitive. The gun, unlike the missile can engage targets at point blank range. It is also faster than the missile in target acquisition; that is, the time taken to locate, identify, and engage the target; and at least 10 rounds of gun ammunition can be fired for the cost of one missile.[9]

Projectiles for use against tanks take various forms. HEAT (High Explosive Anti-Tank) shell makes use of a hollow charge, the explosive being shaped round a thin metal case. The shell bursts outside the tank's armour and the energy of detonation is focused like the light reflected from a parabolic mirror, boring a hole through the plate and expanding inside the tank. HESH (High Explosive Squash Head) makes use of PE (Plastic Explosive) which detonates on contact with armour plate and expands. This transmits a shock wave through the armour causing 'spalling' — a scab of steel is knocked off the inside of the armour which breaks into pieces flying in all directions at high velocity. APDS (Armour Piercing Discarded Sabot) is a kinetic energy shell, consisting of a heavy core carried in a light metal carrier, or sabot, which is discarded when the shell leaves the muzzle of the gun, leaving only a very thin shot with high specific gravity and a kinetic energy which enables it to pierce tank armour. The latest types of APDS are fin-stabilised and are known as APFSDS.[10]

The Rarden gun takes its name from the **R**oyal **A**rmament **R**esearch and **D**evelopment Establishment, **En**field, which was responsible for this brilliant design. It is of 30mm calibre and is described as a single-shot self-loading gun with an automatic fire capability. Most other automatic cannon have a rate of fire which is too great to avoid a wide dispersion of shot; so that they rely for effect on a large volume of fire, the greater part of which is wasted. The aim in this gun was to obtain a greater lethality together with a more economical use of ammunition, in order to engage effectively the very large numbers of armoured personnel carriers and other light armoured vehicles which are likely to be encountered in a future war, and to destroy them with the minimum number of shots at the greatest possible range. For this, its primary role, an APDS round fitted with tracer is to be used, and this will defeat frontally the most heavily armoured personnel carrier at ranges of more than 1,000m. It will also be effective against the side armour of main battle tanks. The gun is also supplied with high explosive ammunition for use against soft targets. Against aircraft its larger calibre and greater accuracy compensates for a rate of fire that is lower than that of smaller calibre weapons. Although intended primarily to fire single shots, it can fire a burst of up to six rounds at a cyclic rate of 90 rounds per minute; two clips of three rounds each fully load the gun, and this is enough for the short span of one air engagement. The Rarden gun is mounted in the Scimitar light tank and the Fox armoured car; 165 rounds being carried in the former.[11]

The 105mm Model 56 (ie 1956) Pack Howitzer was developed in Italy and purchased for the British Army. It can be broken down into 11 loads, of which the heaviest is only 122kg. It is primarily a close support weapon, but it can be converted quickly to an anti-tank role by moving the wheels forward and laying the legs flat, so presenting a low silhouette. The long cranked legs of the split trail have to be folded for towing by its associated Land Rover. Its two main disadvantages are that it has a comparatively short range of 10.5km, and it is not designed for high speed towing over rough country. It is principally for these reasons that it is being replaced by the 105mm Light Gun.[12]

The 105mm Light Gun was produced by the British Ministry of Defence to replace the 105mm Pack Howitzer, and was originally intended mainly for limited war. It entered service with the Royal Artillery in 1975. It is portable by helicopter and can be towed over any country that a four-wheel drive Land Rover can negotiate. It is heavier than the 105mm Pack Howitzer, but it has a range of 17km and a whole family of projectiles backed by a flexible multi-charge system. For travel the barrel can be either folded back over the trail, to make a compact load for towing along a road or carriage in a Hercules transport aircraft, or it can be pointed forward in its normal position for firing when it may be required to go into action quickly. In the latter form it can be lifted by a Puma helicopter. The change from one form to the other takes less than a minute. Two light helicopter loads can be produced by removing the elevating mass (that is, the ordnance, the recoil system, the cradle with trunnions, the balancing gear, and the electric firing gear) from the saddle (a lightweight fabrication on which is mounted the elevating gear). The equipment can be re-assembled with one simple tool in less than 10 minutes. Its low silhouette and fast all-round traverse make it an effective anti-tank gun, and, with an elevation up to 70°, it can be used as a howitzer. The maximum rate of fire is six rounds per minute and the sustained rate three rounds per minute. There are two types of charge; the normal, which embraces a number of increments for high or low angle fire, and 'super' which is a fixed charge for low angle fire only. Both types are contained in brass cartridge cases.[13]

A self-propelled gun, though superficially rather like a tank, is far from being one, because it has to be capable of indirect fire and this needs the advanced mechanical aids and training in their use which are the province of the Royal Artillery. The Abbot 105mm gun is the self-propelled field equipment in general use in the British Army; taking the place of the 5.5in and 25-pounder of World War II. It was the first British SP equipment to be designed as a whole and was intended to fill every role from that of a heavy mortar to a fairly long-range field gun.[14] The complete equipment is an armoured fully-tracked vehicle with a 105mm gun, together with a 7.62mm machine gun in a rotatable cupola in the turret for use against ground troops and aircraft. There is a collapsible screen which is fixed permanently to the top of the vehicle and which is erected so that it can float, when it is propelled through the water by its tracks. The range of the gun is 17km, the rate of fire 10 rounds per minute, the maximum speed 48km per hour, and the operational range 390km. 36 rounds of ammunition are carried on the gun and resupply is from a limber. It is not airportable. Though smaller than its contemporaries, its speed, its mobility, and the high rate of fire of its very lethal gun make it a formidable piece of equipment.[15]

There is a new medium field piece, the 155mm FH 70 (ie Field Howitzer of the 'Seventies) which has been developed jointly by the United Kingdom, Germany, and Italy. It is a trailer-mounted towed equipment; but it has an auxiliary power unit mounted on the front of the carriage which can be used for self-propulsion over short distances. This unit also provides the power for operating the connection to the towing vehicle, and also for steering the small trail wheels and raising the main wheels, when the sole plate has been lowered. It is designed to fire all the standard 155mm ammunition in NATO service, and has a maximum range of 24km with a rate of fire of six rounds per minute. There is also a special shell which is understood to be a sub-calibre fin-stabilised round with a range of over 45km.[16]

Various American equipments are in service with the Royal Artillery. The 155mm M109 SP Gun is the smallest piece in the US Army capable of firing a nuclear shell. It carries flotation bags and wash screens, which are inflated when the vehicle is required to float. Its range is 14.6km, its speed 55km per hour, and its cruising range 120km.[17]

The 8in, or 203mm, M110 SP Howitzer was introduced in 1962. It has a comparatively small and very low chassis and the fighting compartment is not armoured. The engine is in front of the chassis on the right; the driver sitting beside it. It is intended as a general artillery support weapon. Its range is 16.8km, and its speed is 54km/h on roads and 14km/h across country.[18]

The 175mm M107 SP Gun is a mobile heavy equipment with a range of 32.7km and the ability to fire nuclear shells. It has the same chassis, mounting, and components as the M110, only the barrels being different. The long barrel together with a fairly large propellant charge gives the projectile a high muzzle velocity, and hence the great range. Spades at the rear of the chassis are lowered and raised hydraulically. The gun is fired by a long lanyard.[19]

As a light anti-aircraft gun, the Bofors 40mm is a later model of the original version of about 1937, and came into production first in 1951. It has proximity fused ammunition which explodes up to 6.5m away from the target. It has a cyclic rate of fire of 240 rounds per minute and a maximum ceiling of 1,200m. It is mounted on a four-wheel trailer.[20]

The principal tank gun is the 120mm piece of the Chieftain tank. As compared with the previous gun of this calibre mounted in the Conqueror, it does not have the large brass cartridges which pose problems of both storage and post-firing disposal within the confined space of a tank.[21] Separate ammunition is used and the bagged charges are completely combustible. The gun is fully stabilised to allow accurate fire whilst the tank is on the move. The range with APDS is 3,000m and with HESH 8,000m. The rate of fire is seven rounds per minute.[22]

The other tank gun is the 76mm piece mounted in the Scorpion light tank. It can fire HESH or HE at a range of 5,000m, smoke up to 3,700m, and canister with an effective range of 100m. It is fired either by electromechanical means or by a foot pedal.[23]

Guided Weapons

The first generation of guided missile systems trail wires behind them and are steered to their targets by the operator sending signals down the wire by manipulating a small joystick. Second generation missiles also trail wires, but have a semi-automatic guidance, so that the operator only has to keep his sights on the target, establishing a line of sight which is fed into a computer. An infra-red tracker follows an infra-red emission from the missile and, measuring any deviation from the line of sight, sends correcting signals along the trailing wire. Swingfire is an example of the first generation, and HOT, TOW, and MILAN of the second. A third generation, which is not yet in service, will allow the

Above: **Soldiers of The King's Own Royal Border Regiment with self-loading rifles in front of a Chieftain tank.** / *Museum of The Kings's Own Royal Border Regiment*

operator to launch the missile in the general direction of the target and then cease to direct it: hence the term for these missile systems of 'fire and forget'.[24]

Swingfire, though of the first generation is an excellent weapon. Infantry were at first equipped with it, but it is now held only by the Royal Artillery. It is normally mounted in a launcher vehicle, generally a Striker light tank or a FV 438 (based on the FV 432 armoured personnel carrier), but it can also be operated from the ground. Fire control and guidance is effected either from within the vehicle (direct fire) or externally (separated fire) from a position which can be up to 100m from the vehicle or 23m above it. Thus the launcher can be sited under cover while the operator lies concealed in the open. It has a maximum range of 4,000m and a minimum of 150m, and is capable of destroying any existing type of tank. Furthermore, it is virtually immune to electronic counter-measures. With a well-trained gunner, a 90% hit rate is quite common in practice firing.[25]

Until recently, the infantry's anti-tank guided weapon system was Vigilant, man-portable, and wire-guided; and controlled, like Swingfire, by a joystick. It too is lethal against any present main battle tank, and is also immune to electronic countermeasures. It has a range of from 200m to 1,375m.[26] The replacement for Vigilant is the remarkable MILAN, produced by Euromissile, a consortium of the French Aerospatiale company and the German MBB. The name is derived from the French title, **M**issile d'**I**nfanterie **L**eger **An**tichar. It also is wire-guided, but the guidance is semi-automatic, in that the gunner has only to keep the cross-wires of his guidance unit steady on the target during the missile's flight. Further, he has a periscope sight so that he can be under cover from enemy small arms fire. The system consists of a missile in its container and a launch unit. The unit can be rested either on a tripod or on the parapet of a trench with its butt held to the firer's shoulder. It only needs two men, a gunner and a loader. The maximum range is 2,000m, which is the length of the guidance wire, and the minimum range is the arming distance of about 25m. The container, which also serves as a launch type, is mounted on the launch and control unit. As the missile emerges from this tube, the latter is disconnected from the launch unit and thrown backwards. The wings of the missile flick open, imparting a slow spin to it, and it coasts forward for sufficient distance to avoid harm to the gunner, when its sustainer rocket ignites. The time of flight for its maximum range of 2,000m is $12\frac{1}{2}$sec. This is of course

much longer than the time of flight of a shell, which is one of the weaknesses of guided missiles; but, against that, the range of MILAN is comparable to the practicable range of a main battle tank, so that infantry armed with it can engage armour with a reasonable chance of survival. It becomes, therefore, the mainstay of infantry's anti-armour defence.[27]

There are two field anti-aircraft guided missile systems, both equipments of the Royal Artillery. The lighter of these is Blowpipe, which can be carried and operated by one man and is used against low-flying aircraft. There are only two main components, the aiming unit and the missile in its canister. All that is necessary to prepare it for action is to clip the aiming unit on to the canister. The gunner acquires the target in his monocular sight, fires the missile, and controls it towards the target by a thumb-generated controller.[28]

The other system, Rapier, is much bigger. It is a tactical surface to air missile to engage and destroy aircraft flying at supersonic speed, and it replaces Bofors as the main defence against low-level attack. There is a fire unit, an optical tracker, and a power unit. These three are connected to each other by cable and can be sited separately as best suits the conditions. The fire unit is loaded with four missiles and is then left unattended, the system being operated by one gunner at the tracker. The fire unit, in addition to the missile launch mechanism, has a search and acquisition radar. When this detects a target its associated IFF (Identification Friend or Foe) equipment automatically interrogates it. If it is hostile, the tracker operator is alerted and, from the radar data, the tracker is directed towards the target. The operator then sees it in his optical sight, and the missile is automatically commanded to follow an optical or radar sighting to the target. For movement of the equipment, one Land Rover tows the fire unit and carries the tracker and four missiles; whilst a second Land Rover tows a missile re-supply trailer with more missiles.[29]

For air to surface use against tanks, the American TOW (**T**ube **O**perated **W**ire Guided) anti-tank missile system is being fitted to the new Lynx helicopters. The launch motor ejects the missile from the tube, and after flying several metres the flight motor ignites. Commands

35

are transmitted by two wires which uncoil from separate spools. Short wings and rudder surfaces on the missile unfold as it leaves the tube, and provided the operator keeps his sight on the target the missile is bound to hit it. The maximum range is 3,750m.[30]

Lance is the biggest guided weapon equipment on the establishment of the Royal Artillery, and is the main NATO tactical nuclear weapon. It is a supersonic inertially guided ballistic missile with a range of 75 miles. It normally carries a nuclear warhead with a yield in the kiloton range, but it can alternatively carry a conventional HE warhead. It is invulnerable to all known electronic counter-measures. The missile is 20ft long and the entire system comprises four ground support vehicles: a tracked self-propelled launcher (SPL), a tracked loader-transporter (LT), an alternative wheeled 'zero length' more mobile launcher (LZL), and a wheeled mobility unit. The missile is normally carried on and fired from the SPL, which operates in conjunction with the LT. The latter carries two spare missiles which it can reload into the launcher. If desired, missile and launcher can be removed from the SPL and fitted in the LZL, which is lighter and can be towed by a 2-ton vehicle. The mobility unit carries the necessary equipment to effect the transfer. The whole system is easily air-lifted.[31]

Mines and Mine Clearance

The Bar Mine is a formidable anti-tank weapon. The mines are supplied either in a special pack containing 72 mines, which can be loaded in the standard NATO pallet, or in a man-portable pack of four mines. Some 600 to 700 mines can be laid in an hour. The layer incorporates a furrow-forming unit and a conveyor in which the mines are automatically armed before laying. The furrow is made with a coulter and plough, and is closed and levelled after the mine is laid by disc harrows and a trailing chain. The layer can be pulled by a FV 432 armoured personnel carrier, in which it could also be stored, which gives protection to the crew. The long shape of the mine doubles the chance of it being activated by a tank, and its small cross-section enables a trench for buried mines to be produced with a relatively low tractive effort. Minefields with the same equivalent stopping power as those laid with 'conventional' round mines can be provided with half the number of mines. The Bar Mine, which is made with plastic materials and only a few metal parts, is 120cm long and 10.8cm broad.[32]

Against enemy on foot there is the Ranger system of anti-personnel mines. These are intended to disable men, rather than kill them, on the grounds that the removal of wounded men from a minefield presents the enemy with an additional problem. The Ranger launcher can throw 1,296 mines per minute. It can be mounted on the top of an armoured personnel carrier towing a Bar Mine layer, so that anti-personnel mines can be thrown out to cover the anti-tank minefield and deter clearance. It can also be used separately to infest woods, the edges of roads, etc, with the object of canalising the movements of enemy infantry into fire-swept zones. The system consists of 72 disposable tubes placed in the launcher, each tube containing 18 anti-personnel mines. An electrically ignited cartridge expels a tube about 100m, the tubes being fired in turn,. It takes less than six minutes to recharge the launcher.[33]

An ingenious mine-clearance system has the very descriptive name of Giant Viper. It is designed to blast a 24ft wide passage for vehicles through a minefield of up to 200 yards in depth. The principal component is a hose, 250 yards long and $2\frac{5}{8}$in in diameter, filled with a plastic explosive. It is packed in a wooden box mounted on a two-wheeled trailer, which is towed by a tank or an armoured personnel carrier. The hose is propelled across the minefield by a cluster of eight rocket motors, attached to the leading end, which are fired from inside the towing vehicle. Three parachutes are attached to the tail end of the hose, and these straighten it in flight and operate the striker mechanism which detonates the charge after the hose has landed. For the operation the Giant Viper is towed to a firing point about 50 yards from the edge of the minefield, and the trailer is aligned to the required line of flight.[34]

Below left: Soldiers of The King's Own Royal Border Regiment sitting on an armoured personnel carrier, and carrying self-loading rifles. / *Museum of The King's Own Royal Border Regiment*

Below: A soldier of The Argyll and Sutherland Highlanders (Princess Louise's) with a General Purpose machine gun (GPMG) in its light machine gun role on an exercise in Germany. In the background is a Scorpion light tank. / *Crown Copyright*

Right: 'Waiting for the attack'; an Arygll and Sutherland Highlander on Exercise Spearpoint in Germany with a GPMG in its light role. / *Crown Copyright*

Below right: The GPMG on its tripod for sustained fire in its support gun role. / *Crown Copyright*

Tactical Nuclear Weapons

The yields of present NATO nuclear weapons very between about one kiloton and 400 kilotons. From a 10-kiloton explosion casualties to unprotected personnel are likely over an area of two square miles around 'ground zero'. From a 20-kiloton explosion this would be increased to two and a half square miles, and from a 100-kiloton explosion the area affected would be three and a half square miles. (It takes more then 10 times the explosive power, in this case, to double the danger area.) It will be apparent, however, that there are considerable problems in using nuclear weapons when forces are locked in close combat if casualties to one's own side are to be avoided. The Americans are developing a range of very much smaller weapons, known as 'mini-nukes', with yields of as little as 0.1-kilotons. These will have great explosive power, but it will be concentrated over a small area and the residual, or long-lasting, radiation will be negligible. A single shot from such a weapon would destroy such targets as a headquarters, a tank concentration, or a battery of artillery.[35]

Left: The GPMG as a support gun manned by a detachment of The Royal Irish Rangers (27th (Inniskilling), 83rd and 87th). / *Crown Copyright*

Below: A GPMG section of the 1st Battalion The Prince of Wales's Own Regiment of Yorkshire, dug in and wearing NBC (nuclear, biological and chemical) protective suits. / *Crown Copyright*

Right: Firing a GPMG from a concealed position. / *Crown Copyright*

Far right: Private Twentyman of The King's Own Royal Border Regiment taking aim with his GPMG. / *Museum of The King's Own Royal Border Regiment*

Below right: A sergeant of The King's Own Royal Border Regiment firing a GPMG from an armoured personnel carrier. / *Museum of The King's Own Royal Border Regiment*

Above left: A detachment of the 1st Battalion Coldstream Guards on exercise in Germany preparing to open fire with a GPMG in its sustained fire role. / *Crown Copyright*

Left: A GPMG mounted on a 'pulk' during an exercise in Norway. / *Crown Copyright*

Above: The new Individual Weapon, or rifle, with a calibre of 4.85mm. / *Crown Copyright*

Centre right: The new Light Support Weapon, or light machine gun, which, except for a heavier barrel and a bipod, is practically the same as the Individual Weapon. / *Crown Copyright*

Below right: The Light Support Weapon being fired with its bipod raised. / *Crown Copyright*

Above: **A soldier of The King's Own Royal Border Regiment loading an 81mm mortar on an APC.** / *Museum of The King's Own Royal Border Regiment*

Right: **A mortar detachment of the Coldstream Guards preparing to fire an 81mm mortar.** / *Crown Copyright*

Left: An 81mm mortar of the 1st Battalion Coldstream Guards being fired. / Crown Copyright

Below: An 81mm mortar being loaded in an AFV 432 armoured personnel carrier during an exercise in Germany by the Coldstream Guards. / Crown Copyright

Left: Infantrymen preparing to fire a 2in mortar. / *Crown Copyright*

Below: Soldiers of the 1st Battalion The Queen's Regiment preparing a Wombat for firing on the range at Suffield, Alberta, Canada. APCs are in the background. / *Crown Copyright*

Left: Soldiers of The Royal Regiment of Wales (24th/41st Foot) training with a Wombat in Germany. / *Crown Copyright*

Below: A side view of The Royal Regiment of Wales Wombat detachment. / *Crown Copyright*

Left: Close-up view of a Wombat of the anti-tank platoon, Somme Company of the 1st Battalion The King's Own Royal Border Regiment, manned by Corporal D. B. Hall. / *Museum of The King's Own Royal Border Regiment*

Below: A detachment of the 1st Battalion The King's Own Royal Border Regiment with a Wombat in action. / *Museum of The King's Own Royal Border Regiment*

Bottom: A Wombat mounted on a AFV 432 APC of The Duke of Edinburgh's Royal Regiment (Berkshire and Wiltshire). / *Crown Copyright*

Above: A detachment of The King's Own Royal Border Regiment preparing a Wombat as an underslung load for a Royal Air Force helicopter. / *Museum of The King's Own Royal Border Regiment*

Right: Sergeant Rawcliffe of the Reconnaissance Platoon, 1st Battalion The King's Own Royal Border Regiment checking a batch of practice rounds for Wombat. Note the Eager Beaver forklift truck doing the loading. / *Museum of The King's Own Royal Border Regiment*

Top: **A soldier of The King's Own Royal Border Regiment with the Carl Gustav anti-tank recoilless rifle.** / *Museum of The King's Own Royal Border Regiment*

Above: **The 105mm Pack Howitzer.** / *Crown Copyright*

Top right: **A 105mm Pack Howitzer of the Royal Regiment of Artillery and its detachment.** / *Crown Copyright*

Above right: **A section of 105mm Pack Howitzers which saw service in the Radfan, Aden and Borneo.** / *Crown Copyright*

Right: **The 105mm Light Gun.** / *Crown Copyright*

Right: The 105mm Light Gun from the rear, showing the design for recoil at extreme elevation. / Crown Copyright

Below: A 105mm Light Gun with its Royal Artillery detachment. / Crown Copyright

Left: A 105mm Light Gun ready to fire at a high angle of elevation. / *Crown Copyright*

Below: 105mm Light Guns firing on Salisbury Plain February 1978. / *Crown Copyright*

Above far left: A 105mm Light Gun being prepared for lifting by a Puma helicopter of the Royal Air Force. / *Crown Copyright*

Above left: The Puma helicopter carrying the 105mm Light Gun. / *Crown Copyright*

Left: A 105mm Light Gun being off-loaded from a C-130 Hercules aircraft of the RAF. / *Crown Copyright*

Above: A 105mm Light Gun in the towing position. / *Crown Copyright*

Below: The famous 25-pounder which saw service throughout World War II and in Korea. It is still used for training purposes. / *Crown Copyright*

Left: The 5.5in medium gun, which is shortly to be replaced by the FH70 155mm.
/ *Crown Copyright*

Below left: A 105mm Abbot self-propelled gun.
/ *Crown Copyright*

Right: A 105mm Abbot SP gun on the move.
/ *Crown Copyright*

Below: The 155mm medium field equipment of the Royal Artillery, the FH70. / *Crown Copyright*

Top: The 155mm FH70 in the towing position. / *Crown Copyright*

Above: The 155mm FH70 coming into action after being towed. / *Crown Copyright*

Above right: The 155mm FH70 being propelled by its own auxiliary power unit. / *Crown Copyright*

Right: The 155mm FH70 with gun detachment, preparing to fire. / *Crown Copyright*

Left: **A 155mm FH70 showing split trail and mounting.** / *Crown Copyright*

Below left: **A 155mm FH70 firing.** / *Crown Copyright*

Right: **A 155mm FH70 firing at extreme elevation.** / *Crown Copyright*

Below: **The American 155mm M109 SP Gun.** / *Crown Copyright*

Left: The 155mm M109 SP Gun at a high angle of elevation. / *Crown Copyright*

Below left: M109 SP Guns of 45 Medium Regiment, Royal Artillery, on parade in Germany. / *Crown Copyright*

Right: Breech end and loading equipment of a M109 gun: 27 Medium Regiment Royal Artillery. / *Crown Copyright*

Below: An M109 SP Gun of the Royal Artillery on display at the Royal School of Artillery, Larkhill. / *Crown Copyright*

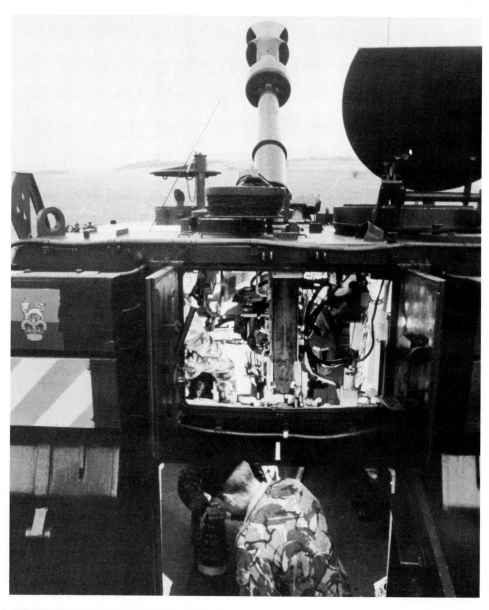

Left: Rear view of a M109 155mm SP gun. / *Crown Copyright*

Below: The American M110 SP 8in Howitzer. / *Crown Copyright*

Right: The M110 SP 8in Howitzer, with its Royal Artillery detachment, ready to fire. / *Crown Copyright*

Below right: A M107 175mm SP Gun of Q (Sanna's Post) Battery, Royal Artillery, of 5 Regiment in Germany. / *Crown Copyright*

Left: M107mm SP Gun at a high angle of elevation. / Crown Copyright

Below: Bofors L70/40mm anti-aircraft gun of 16 Light Air Defence Regiment, Royal Artillery. / Crown Copyright

Above: An L70/40mm Gun being fired at night by 22 Light Air Defence Regiment, Royal Artillery. / *Crown Copyright*

Left: Swingfire being demonstrated by Staff Sergeant P. Wainman and Corporal C. Pyrah of The King's Own Border Regiment. / *Museum of The King's Own Border Regiment*

Above left: **Soldiers of The King's Own Royal Border Regiment with Swingfire.** / *Museum of The King's Own Royal Border Regiment*

Left: **The Swingfire anti-tank guided missile system fitted in the Striker CVR.** / *Crown Copyright*

Above: **A Swingfire missile immediately after firing from an AFV 438.** / *Crown Copyright*

Right: **Soldiers of The Royal Irish Rangers about to fire Vigilant.** / *Crown Copyright*

Left: MILAN: a side view of the latest infantry anti-tank guided weapon. / *Crown Copyright*

Below far left: MILAN: a view from the front of this remarkable and revolutionary weapon. / *Crown Copyright*

Below left: MILAN: ready for transporting by its two-man crew. / *Crown Copyright*

Right: MILAN: ready to fire. / *Crown Copyright*

Below: Blowpipe: the Royal Artillery light anti-aircraft guided missile; shown with its team in a slit trench. / *Crown Copyright*

Above: Blowpipe: ready to fire from the shoulder in the standing position. A second missile in its canister lies on the ground. / *Crown Copyright*

Left: A Blowpipe troop of the Royal Artillery, attached to a battalion of The Royal Anglian Regiment, preparing to fire in Northern Norway. / *Crown Copyright*

Above right: The Rapier tactical surface to air missile of The Royal Artillery: the fire unit loaded with its four missiles. / *Crown Copyright*

Right: Rapier: the fire unit from the rear with two missiles loaded. / *Crown Copyright*

Above: A detachment loading a Rapier fire unit with its four missiles. / *Crown Copyright*

Left: A frontal view of a Rapier fire unit with two missiles loaded. / *Crown Copyright*

Left: A Rapier missile in flight. / *Crown Copyright*

Below: A Lance missile of the Royal Artillery ready for firing. Lance is the main NATO tactical nuclear weapon. / *Crown Copyright*

Left: Sappers of the 26th Engineer Regiment, Corps of Royal Engineers, clearing a safe lane through a minefield. / *Crown Copyright*

Below: A sapper of the Royal Engineers arming a Mark VII anti-tank mine. *Crown Copyright*

Right: A detachment of the 26th Engineer Regiment laying Bar Mines. The Bar Mine layer is being towed by an AFV 432, on top of which is mounted a Ranger anti-personnel mine launcher. The sappers can be seen feeding Bar Mines on to the conveyor belt feed. / *Crown Copyright*

Below right: A Ranger anti-personnel mine launcher mounted on a Stalwart amphibian. / *Crown Copyright*

9

Armoured Fighting Vehicles

The main battle tank is, in chess terms, the queen of the battlefield. It is a mobile armoured fortress which is the spearhead of the attack and the buttress of the defence. Indeed, the roles of each of the chess board pieces bear some vague resemblance to the various fighting elements of the modern army: the castles perhaps representing artillery; the bishops, light tanks and armoured cars; the knights, helicopters; and the invaluable pawns, of course, the infantry.

The ideal battle tank would have armour plating capable of withstanding all shells and guided missiles; an armament composed of a gun powerful enough to knock out any hostile battle tank, together with a machine gun for ranging and another for use against aircraft and men in the open; a fire control system and rangefinder that will ensure a hit with the gun's first round; the ability to move across country at high speed and to traverse rivers; the capacity to fight at night; immunity against nuclear, biological and chemical attack; and reasonable comfort for its crew.[1] The ideal tank, however, does not exist and never will, because factors such as the maximum permissible weight and size impose compromises in one or more aspects. High speed may entail sacrifice in the thickness of armour or the calibre of gun. To strike the right balance is always difficult: a high cross-country speed, for instance, is obviously not worth while if the crew is so shaken as to impair their fighting efficiency. Of main battle tanks in service at the time of writing, the British Chieftain probably embodies the best achievable blend of the various primary factors; though how it will compare with such new tanks as the German Leopard 2, the American XM-1, and the Russian T-72 remains to be seen.

The first Chieftains entered service in 1963, and they were followed in 1966 by the Mark II with a more powerful engine of 650hp, and in 1969 by the Mark III with an even more powerful engine. Now there is the Mark V in which the engine has again been increased in power and which carries a greater amount of ammunition. This latest mark has a road speed of 30mph and a road range of 300 miles. The 120mm gun, which constitutes its main armament has already been described, and there are 53 rounds of mixed ammunition, including HESH, APDS, and smoke. For secondary armament there are two 7.62mm General Purpose machine guns, one coaxially mounted and the other on the commander's cupola for anti-aircraft fire; there is also 12.7mm Browning machine gun, coaxially mounted for ranging and adapted to fire in bursts of three rounds. On either side of the turret is a bank of six discharger cups to fire smoke grenades for close protection at short range. They are operated electrically and form an almost instantaneous smoke screen. A searchlight is mounted coaxially with the gun which can produce both infra-red and white light. The engine has six forward and two reverse gears, and an auxiliary engine drives a generator to serve the electrical systems. The interior can be completely sealed off to give protection against nuclear, biological and chemical warfare, and with its hatches sealed the tank can operate for long periods under such conditions. In addition to the searchlight, the Chieftain tank has a lavish range of appliances for night vision, including infra-red filtered head lamps, infra-red sights for commander and gunner, and a viewer for the driver. The

frontal arc has an armour thickness of about 150mm, sloping at an angle of 60°. This has added considerably to its weight, but it is maintained that any advantage that the German Leopard tank may obtain from increased speed at the expense of armour is offset by the buffeting which the crew would get if the maximum speed is attempted over an uneven surface. The incorporation of an engine to provide the same speed with the heavier armour and without increasing the overall size of the tank might impair the all-round traverse of the turret, and thus hamper the ability to engage those unexpected targets that appear so frequently during mobile operations.[2]

As regards the threat from anti-tank guided missiles, the tank has certain compensating advantages. It can produce a much faster rate of fire, both by day and night, and in all kinds of weather. The guided missile, on the other hand, is as accurate as the tank at ranges of 1,500m and less, and more accurate at the longer ranges up to 4,000m. At 2,000m and below the Chieftain is as likely to get a hit with the first round of its 120mm gun as is a guided missile, so that it remains the best of all anti-tank weapons.[3]

Another attribute of the tank is that, because the interior can be sealed, it can move and fight freely when tactical nuclear weapons are being used; in an environment, therefore, in which other troops could not survive. This attribute of the battle tank is shared, too, by a number of other armoured fighting vehicles.

The Scorpion Family

This group of tracked armoured vehicles constitutes one of the more remarkable developments of recent times. The same chassis, and as many other parts as possible are common to seven different types of vehicle: Scorpion, a light tank armed with a 76mm gun; Scimitar, also a light tank but armed with a 30mm Rarden gun; Striker, an anti-tank guided missile vehicle; Spartan, an armoured personnel carrier; Sultan, a command vehicle; Samson, an armoured recovery vehicle; and Samaritan, an armoured ambulance. All these are built by Alvis of Coventry, in conjunction with the Ministry of Defence and the Military Vehicles and Engineering Establishment (MVEE).

In the late 1950s planning started to replace the Saladin (armoured car), Saracen (armoured personnel carrier, wheeled), and Ferret scout car. It was first intended that there should be a single vehicle — the Combat Vehicle Reconnaissance (CVR), capable of carrying out the tasks of reconnaissance, fire support, and anti-tank action. However, to achieve the mobility aimed at there had to be a weight limit of 18,000lb, so that two vehicles could be carried in a C130 Hercules transport aircraft. This made it impossible to provide sufficient space in one armoured vehicle for the weapons, equipment, and crew for all three of the above roles. It was decided, therefore, to have three types of armoured vehicle for these tasks, and four others for command, surveillance, recovery, and medical. All have light steel tracks with rubber bushes and pads to give them a cross-country performance, and special light aluminium armour for protection against small arms fire and shell fragments.

Scorpion is a fast light tank — perhaps the smallest and fastest in service anywhere — and the first tracked reconnaissance vehicle to be made entirely of aluminium. Its speed across country and its small size enables it to move rapidly in and out of the cover provided by even small folds in the ground, making it ideal for armed reconnaissance and rearguard actions. Owing to its narrow width it can use paths and forest tracks impassable to Chieftain. Scorpion, and other members of the family, can be dropped from the air with the aid of four parachutes and a shock absorber platform. A wading screen can be erected quickly, enabling it to float, and it can be propelled through the water by its own tracks at a speed of 4mph. This can be increased to 6mph by bolting on propeller units. Having a ground pressure less than that of a man walking, it can cross bog, soft sand, and paddy fields, can traverse a class 10 bridge, and can climb a gradient of 1 in 2.

Scorpion's main armament is the 76mm gun, mounted in a turret with all-round traverse. A 7.62mm General Purpose machine gun is mounted coaxially for ranging, and there are two multi-barrel smoke dischargers, one each side of the turret. The gun's HESH ammunition is capable of dealing with medium armour up to 3,500 yards and it is effective against the side armour and tracks of most battle tanks. 40 rounds, all fixed ammunition, are carried in easily accessible bins. In the turret a commander/loader and a gunner/radio operator sit either side of the main armament. The driver is the remaining man of the crew. At the rear of the fighting compartment is mounted a NBC filtration pack which ensures clean air under pressure. The maximum speed is 50mph, the road range is over 400 miles, track life is normally over 3,000 miles, and major maintenance is needed every 3,000 miles or once a year, whichever comes first.

Scorpion is the medium reconnaissance equipment of armoured reconnaissance regiments and is very popular with all ranks.[4]

Scimitar is also a fast light tank, and very similar to Scorpion, except that its main armament is the 30mm Rarden gun, though mounted in the same turret. It has been designed for close reconnaissance, and though it is part of the equipment of the armoured reconniassance regiments, Scimitar armed troops are deployed to battle groups as their close reconnaissance force. Its main target is the hostile armoured personnel carrier, and other light armoured vehicles at ranges of 1,000 metres and more; and its main purpose reconnaissance and security. The small calibre of the Rarden gun has the great advantage that a large amount of ammunition can be carried in the vehicle. Empty shell cases are ejected

Below: **Chieftain tanks passing the saluting base on the Royal Review in Germany.** / *Crown Copyright*

to the outside, so that the turret is not cluttered with them nor affected by powder fumes. A 7.62mm machine gun is coaxially mounted in the turret and multi-barrel smoke dischargers are fitted, one each side of it. Other details are the same as for Scorpion.[5]

Striker has been designed as a missile-armed main battle tank destroyer, fitted with the Swingfire system with a range of 4,000m, and is issued to anti-tank batteries of the Royal Artillery. Five Swingfire missiles are carried in launcher bins on the roof, and five more inside the vehicle. A box hull has been provided to give more internal space. The launchers are elevated hydraulically for firing; and aiming, firing, and re-loading are all carried out under armour. There is a 7.62mm machine gun mounted on the cupola, and multi-barrel smoke dischargers are fitted, one each side of the hull. Striker could be employed in support of the armoured reconnaissance regiment.[6]

Spartan is designed primarily to fulfill the roles of either an armoured personnel carrier or a surveillance vehicle, and it forms part of the equipment of an armoured reconnaissance regiment. As an APC it can carry an assault section of a commander and four men, in addition to driver and gunner, and for surveillance it is equipped with the ZB 296 radar, as well as various infra-red and other night detection devices. In the Royal Artillery it is fitted to carry the Blowpipe anti-aircraft missile system, and, thus equipped, it provides defence for the battle groups against low flying aircraft. In its APC role it has stowage for weapons, equipment, mines, explosives and other stores. There is a 7.62mm machine gun in a rotating cupola, and hatches in the hull allow the crew to use their personal weapons at the sides and rear. The assault section enter and leave by a door at the rear. Maximum speed is 50mph and the range is 300 miles.[7]

Sultan is an armoured command vehicle for use at the headquarters of battle groups, regiments and battalions. It has 12in higher sides than the Spartan to give more room inside for radio sets, map boards, and additional batteries; and a pent house can be erected at the rear to afford greater accommodation for the battle group and other staffs at the halt. Side tents can also be fitted for a prolonged stay. Four radio sets can be operated from the vehicle, but the normal is two — for a command net and a rear link. Overhead and to the left is a pintle-mounted 7.62mm General Purpose machine gun on a cupola with an all round traverse, the maximum road speed is 45mph, and the road range is 300 miles.[8]

Samson is an armoured recovery vehicle, with the same hull as Spartan, but with a heavy duty winch and other equipment for the recovery of any vehicle in the Scorpion family. REME Light Aid Detachments attached to units having vehicles of that family are equipped with Samsons. As armament the Samson has a pintle-mounted General

Below: Chieftain tanks of the 4/7th Royal Dragoon Guards taking up firing positions in the Suffield Training Area, near Medicine Hat, Southern Alberta, Canada. (The training area consists of 1,000 square miles of high rolling plateau, but it has only five trees!) / *Crown Copyright*

Purpose machine gun and two multi-barrelled smoke dischargers. The winch is driven from the main engine and it is powerful enough to pull vehicles across a river.[9]

The last of this family of tracked vehicles is the Samaritan, the armoured ambulance. It carries a commander, a medical orderly, and a driver, and can accommodate four stretcher or sitting cases, or two of each. It has the same hull as the Samson and there is an air cooler in the casualty compartment. The armoured reconnaissance regiments and some other units are equipped with Samaritans.[10]

The Fox armoured car is a development of the very successful Ferret scout car. It was designed to meet the need for a wheeled reconnaissance vehicle of light weight for roles which included armed reconnaissance, internal security, and escorts. It has a turret with all-round traverse and it is armed with the Rarden gun, as well as a coaxially mounted 7.62mm General Purpose machine gun and smoke dischargers. It also has day and night sighting and vision instruments. For a wheeled vehicle it has excellent cross-country ability, and it can ford water one metre deep and swim under its own power with the aid of rapidly erected flotation equipment. Hull and turret are constructed of a light alloy armour. A Hercules C130 aircraft can carry three cars, or two if they are to be dropped by parachute. The car is powered by the same engine as Scorpion and has a top speed of 66mph. Other attributes include power-assisted steering, run-flat tyres, and a five-speed pre-selecting gearbox, with a transfer box providing reversal of all five speeds. The drive is transmitted through a fluid coupling on to all four wheels. The crew consists of a commander/loader, a gunner/operator, and a driver.[11] Certain Regular and TAVR reconnaissance regiments have Fox armoured cars as part of their equipment.

The Ferret scout car was developed between 1951 and 1953 from the Daimler scout car, a very popular vehicle. It is used mainly for liaison and similar tasks, and is armed with a .3in Browning machine gun in a turret. The units to which Ferrets are issued include armoured reconnaissance regiments and mechanised infantry battalions.

The FV 432 tracked armoured personnel carrier has been the standard equipment of the mechanised infantry battalions since 1964. It carries a commander, a driver, and a section of 10 men. It has a road speed of 32mph and a range of 360 miles. A collapsible screen can be erected in one minute to enable it to float and move through the water under its own power. It is armed with a 7.62mm General Purpose machine gun, which is pintle-mounted on the roof. The section enter and leave by a door at the rear. Other vehicles on the same chassis include the Abbot SP gun, the FV 434 recovery vehicle, the FV 436 with Green Archer mortar locating radar, and the FV 438 with Swingfire. The FV 432 itself can also be easily adapted to such other roles as the carriage of Wombat and crew, the carriage of the 81mm mortar, an artillery observation post, and similar uses.[12]

There are two notable examples of the Chieftain hull being used for other purposes. One of these is the Armoured Vehicle-Launched Bridge, FV 4205, by which a Class 60 bridge is launched hydraulically without the crew being exposed. It is the No 8 Tank Bridge and has a span of 22.9m. The other is the Armoured Recovery Vehicle, FV 4204, which has two winches and a hydraulically-operated earth anchor-blade. It is armed with a 7.62mm machine gun and smoke dischargers.[13]

Left: A Chieftain tank of the Royal Armoured Corps, acting as 'enemy' on an exercise in Germany, and without its skirting boards. In the background is Schloss Marienburg. / *Crown Copyright*

Below left: Scorpion light tanks on the 1977 Royal Review in Germany. The Scorpions are armed with the 76mm gun. / *Crown Copyright*

Right: Scorpion light tanks of the Royal Armoured Corps and Gazelle helicopters of the Army Air Corps at the Royal Review of 1977 in Germany. / *Crown Copyright*

Below: Scimitar light tanks with their Rarden guns passing the saluting base on the Royal Review, followed by AFV 438s equipped with Swingfires. / *Crown Copyright*

Left: A Scimitar belonging to a close reconnaissance troop of the 13th/18th Royal Hussars (Queen Mary's Own) on exercise in Germany with the 1st Battalion The Prince of Wale's Own Regiment of Yorkshire.

Below: Striker; one of the Scorpion family of 'Combat Vehicles Reconnaissance Tracked' (CVR(T)), to give the official name. It is armed with five Swingfire missiles, carried in launchers bins on the roof, with five more inside. / *Crown Copyright*

Right: Spartan: another of the Scorpion family. This is used either as an armoured personnel carrier or, with its radar, as a surveillance vehicle. / *Crown Copyright*

Below right: A Spartan on an exercise in Germany. Note the trackway over which it is moving. / *Crown Copyright*

Above: Sultan, the armoured command vehicle of the Scorpion family. It is intended for the headquarters of battle groups, regiments, and battalions, and is fitted with the Clansman type radio sets. / *Crown Copyright*

Left: Spartan as a Royal Artillery command vehicle on exercise in Germany. / *Crown Copyright*

Above right: Samson, the armoured recovery vehicle in the Scorpion range. It is intended primarily for the recovery of Scorpion and her sisters, but can be used for any recovery within its 12ton pull limit. / *Crown Copyright*

Right: Samaritan; the Scorpion type armoured ambulance, with accommodation for four stretcher cases or four sitting wounded. / *Crown Copyright*

Left: A Fox armoured car crossing a water obstacle. Note the Rarden gun in the turret. / *Crown Copyright*

Below: A Swingfire anti-tank missile being fired from a Mark V Ferret scout car by C Squadron The Life Guards during an exercise in Norway. / *Crown Copyright*

Right: AFV 432 APCs of the 2nd Battalion The Royal Irish Rangers in the 'enemy' role during an exercise in Germany. / *Crown Copyright*

Below right: A battalion headquarters of The Royal Scots (The Royal Regiment) moving in AFV 432 APCs on an exercise in Germany with a Sioux helicopter of the Army Air Corps overhead. The APCs are named after some of the Regiment's battle honours. The Commanding Officer's APC is Corunna, and the leading one on the right is Waterloo, followed by St Sebastian. / *Crown Copyright*

Above left: Soldiers of The Royal Irish Rangers disembarking from AFV 432 APCs. The AFV 432 in the background is armed with the 30mm Rarden gun. / Crown Copyright

Left: A Chieftain bridgelayer on exercises in Germany. / Crown Copyright

Above: A Chieftain bridgelayer in action in Germany. / Crown Copyright

Right: A Chieftain crossing a bridge laid by a Centurion bridgelayer during an exercise in Germany. / Crown Copyright

10

The Army Helicopter

The army helicopter is a vehicle so new in warfare that it requires rather fuller treatment than has been accorded the armoured fighting vehicles described in the previous chapter; for tanks and armoured cars have a history of two world wars behind them, whilst it was not till the early 1960s that helicopters formed a significant part of the equipment of the Army Air Corps — itself only created in 1957.

It will be appreciated from its title that this chapter is concerned with the army helicopter only. The reason for this is that, unlike the practice in the other two Services, the helicopter is not used by the Army as an aircraft, but rather, as it has been well described, as 'a ground vehicle which has the capability of lifting off the ground and moving rapidly forwards, backwards, or sideways.'[1] In battle, indeed, the armed helicopter fires its missiles from a stationary position at tree top level — a position in no way dissimilar to that of an infantry Milan team perched precariously on a platform in the upper branches.

The helicopter was first used by British forces during the counter-insurgency operations in Malaya. It proved an admirable means of reconnaissance in difficult country, and it soon showed its value for the rapid evacuation of casualties; and this in turn led to transport forward — the rapid deployment of troops, in place of the slow trudge to positions through thick jungle. This last, however, was limited because of the inability of the low-powered helicopters of the time to lift many men.

In the operations against Egypt in 1956, 45 Commando, Royal Marines, was put ashore by 16 Whirlwind helicopters of the Joint Experimental Helicopter Unit (JEHU), operating from a carrier standing 15 miles off the coast. They were commanded by a lieutenant-colonel and were flown by Army and RAF pilots.[2]

In Algeria in 1958 the French Army made extensive use of helicopters for the movement of troops. They proved so vulnerable, however, to small arms fire that a number of Alouette helicopters were fitted with rockets and machine guns to provide armed escorts, while other Alouettes were used as command posts. Thus the conception of an attack helicopter originated in the French Army.[3]

In 1961 the United States of America became involved militarily in Vietnam, and this campaign really marked the rise of the helicopter as a standard army fighting and reconnaissance vehicle. During the course of the fighting there were remarkable developments in helicopter technology and tactics. Initially, their primary role was as troop carriers, but the increasing effectiveness of enemy action against them forced the US Army to give them some defensive armament, and then to develop a fighting helicopter as escort. This at first was a light reconnaissance machine fitted with a 7.62mm 'minigun', housed in a pod and firing either 2,000 or 4,000 rounds per minute. The next step was to attach various armament systems to a standard utility helicopter (a method still widely favoured today). The UH-1C of this type had a minigun and seven rocket tube launchers. This was very successful, but it had the disadvantage that, with the pilot and gunner seated side by side, it presented a wide frontal aspect which was tactically undesirable, and the

aerodynamic drag from this and the exterior armament affected performance. In 1966, therefore, the Bell AH (ie Attack Helicopter)-1G was brought into service. It was designed specifically as a fighting machine, and known as the Huey Cobra. Its armament comprised a turret equipped with a 7.62mm minigun and a 40mm grenade launcher, capable of 400 anti-personnel rounds per minute, as well as wing-mounted 2.75in rockets with 17lb warheads. Other weapons could be substituted to deal with different types of target; but all these weapons were suited to the particular requirements of the Vietnam war. A notable development in 1972 was the fitting of the TOW missile system to some of the Cobras. The Australian forces in Vietnam also used armed helicopters of American pattern, but they preferred the UH-1H utility helicopter with a 'button-on' weapon system because they could buy two of these for the cost of one Cobra.[4]

In the 1960s the Army Air Corps of the British Army replaced its Auster fixed wing aircraft by light helicopters. Its major equipment eventually became the Sioux, which was the Bell 47 built under licence by Westland, and a larger helicopter, the Scout. The Sioux, used for battlefield reconnaissance, can carry three people, including the pilot, at a speed of about 70kts (80mph). Loads up to 600lb can be underslung. It is powered by a single petrol engine. The Scout is a general utility helicopter, carrying four French SS11 wire guided missiles when used in an anti-tank role. In its utility role it can carry six people, including the pilot. It cruises at 100kts (115mph), and is powered by a single gas turbine engine. Up to 1,400lb can be underslung from the hook.[5]

For the American Army, warfare in Europe posed a problem quite different to that encountered in Vietnam; for the principal threat in conventional war lies in the Warsaw Pact's massive superiority in main battle tanks, and hence the likelihood of enemy armoured columns penetrating the NATO defences. From experience in Vietnam, the armed helicopter provides an obvious means of marshalling anti-tank weapons rapidly in the path of an armoured break through.

In 1972 some remarkable tests were carried out at Ansbach in Germany. American Huey Cobra helicopters attacked German Leopard tanks and American Vulcan air defence vehicles. The Vulcan system embraces the 20mm six-barrel anti-aircraft gun which can fire at the rate of 1,000 or 3,000 rounds per minute, the shot being dispersed in a pattern which can be varied by fitting different muzzle adaptors. The Leopards, Vulcans and Cobras had laser receivers attached to them which caused a smoke indicator to explode when a hit would have been registered. At the end of about 60 tests only 10 helicopters had been destroyed by anti-aircraft fire, whereas 167 tanks and 29 Vulcans had been knocked out.[6] Of course it is impossible to say how a test carried out under necessarily rather artificial conditions reflects accurately what would happen in war. Nevertheless, it does show that in the armed helicopter the battle tanks faces a very formidable foe indeed.

Two different policies with regard to armed helicopters vie for support amongst Western Allies. The Americans favour the specially designed attack helicopter. In 1975 a new version of the Cobra was produced, the AH-1Q which incorporated the TOW missile. Its success led to the conversion of all the earlier AH-1Gs into the TOW-mounting AH-1Ss. In the US Army in Europe each division now has two attack helicopter companies, and in due course each corps will have an attack helicopter battalion. The AH-1S can carry up to eight TOW missiles, and will in due course be equipped also with 30mm cannon. Alternatively, 2.75in folding fin aerial rockets can be mounted with a variety of warheads.[7]

The Germans appear to have been attracted by the idea of the special attack helicopter. The British and French, on the other hand, have come down firmly against it and prefer, like the Australians in Vietnam, to fit weapons to their standard helicopters — the British to the utility helicopter and the French to both utility and reconnaissance types.[8]

In 1967 Westland Helicopters and the French helicopter company, Aerospatiale, with the sanction of the British and French Governments, signed an agreement to develop and produce three types of helicopter. The smallest of these is the Gazelle, of French design; the next size is the Lynx, designed by Westland; and the largest is the Puma, also French designed. The Gazelle replaces the Sioux in the Army Air Corps, and began coming into squadron service in 1974. It is powered by a single gas turbine engine and can cruise at up to 130knots (134mph). It can carry five people, including the pilot, and 1,340lb load underslung. It has a ducted tail rotor which improves its cruise performance. On maintenance it is a great improvement on its predecessors because it needs only three hours' maintenance in the field for every hour that it flies, as compared with the four hours required by the Sioux and Scout.[9] The Lynx replaces the Scout as the Army Air Corps' standard utility helicopter, and this very fine machine started coming into Army service in 1977. It is powered by twin gas turbine engines and has an extremely good performance, with a cruising speed of up to 156kts (162mph). In its utility role it can carry the pilot and 10 passengers, or an underslung load of 3,000lb, for its anti-tank role it is equipped with TOW anti-tank guided weapons. British policy is to use armed helicopters primarily against tanks in European warfare, so that weapons additional to TOW are not required. This policy may, however, change as the Soviet helicopter threat increases.[10]

Lynx is comprehensively equipped for bad weather and night operations. It has an Integrated Navigational System to enable it to fly in bad weather. The pilot's display gives him the latitude and longitude, or grid coordinates, of his position. The pilot may also feed in before take-off up to ten destination points, and during flights these destination points can be presented to him in appropriate selection as well as their range and bearing.[11] These facilities are of particular value on account of the Russian fondness of using the cover of bad weather to launch attacks in the hope that this will give them some protection against air attack.[12]

Westland believe that the Lynx has the speed and manoeuvrability to carry out many but not all of the tasks of which a specialised attack helicopter is capable. This of course is true, but, as stated above, it is not the present British opinion that the vastly greater expense of the latter is justified; particularly as attack helicopters are not suited to the utility role and would have to be an addition to the helicopter fleet. Nevertheless, in case there should be a change in this policy, Westland have designed an attack helicopter with armament comparable to that of the Cobra but much faster. There is a weapons bay with separately hinged doors, on the inside of which are mounted the missiles, and which would be swung open before firing. Having all the armament carried inside, the clean exterior, Westland believe, would allow a speed of about 200mph;[13] but it is doubtful in the extreme that this formidable helicopter will ever be built. No doubt it has been argued that the expensive TOW missile is not needed against light tanks and armoured personnel carriers, which can be destroyed by the Rarden gun; but the balance of expense would still be against the Westland project. A strong point in favour of the utility helicopter is that it can be used as such until the moment arrives for fitting its missiles.[14]

Because the armed helicopter has never been used in warfare in Europe, or indeed between first class opponents elsewhere, there is little tactical history to support theories as to the best way of using armed helicopters to halt the progress of enemy armoured columns. There is no doubt, however, that they present the fastest means of massing an anti-tank defence against an armoured penetration. Since this is probably the greatest danger in a conventional war, it follows that the armed helicopters, of which, in the British Army at any rate, there will never be enough, should be held in reserve for this task. It would be quite wrong, therefore, to use the armed helicopters in an offensive search for targets. In so far as this is done from the air, it is a task for the Royal Air Force, and particularly for the Harrier, an aircraft well-suited to the search and

destroy type of mission on close-support targets at the Forward Edge of the Battle Area (FEBA) or in tactical interdiction to the enemy's immediate rear; probably in both cases using the very lethal 'cluster' bomb which contains a large number of bomblets, each capable of penetrating the armour of any tank at present in service.[15]

The helicopter is of course a very vulnerable target — if found. There are a number of factors, however, which aid its concealment. From the air, the notoriously bad flying weather in Europe makes it more difficult for fixed wing aircraft to find and attack a helicopter; and the latter, flying close to the ground, in the 'nap of the earth', melting into the greens and brown of the background, and helped perhaps by cloud and shadow, is a difficult object to sight in the best of conditions. Concealment from ground observation can often be obtained by the cover of trees, the contours of the ground, and even buildings.

Because it is so vulnerable, a helicopter would not be employed beyond the FEBA, where it would expect to encounter the mass of the enemy's ground to air missiles. It could not, therefore, replace the main battle tank in the attack or counter-attack; but it can supplement it in defence by the speed at which helicopters can move to intercept armoured columns, and perhaps hold them till the reserve battle groups arrive to block the enemy's path. This sort of fighting is ideal for the armed helicopters; that is, attacking tanks that are on the move and on ground of the helicopter commander's own choosing.[16]

Field tests were carried out by the American Army, in conjunction with German and Canadian forces, to try and assess the best tactics to adopt in conducting an operation of the above type. The conclusions were that they should always operate in the nap of the earth and should fire from hover at the maximum range of their missiles, using the features of the ground if possible to give them cover from enemy view. Reconnaissance helicopters and armed helicopters should, it was considered, operate together in hunter-killer teams; the reconnaissance helicopters locating the enemy and selecting firing positions, in ambush if possible, to which they would lead the armed helicopters.[17] British trials have confirmed these conclusions, which have now become the accepted tactical doctrine. The modern British concept is to divide the available helicopter force into a number of attack teams of, say, six missile-armed helicopters and two reconnaissance and control helicopters. Immediately after information of an enemy breakthrough, the reconnaissance helicopters would be on the fly line keeping the situation under surveillance. When the Lynx anti-tank helicopter fire teams are tasked to attack the enemy armour, they fly very low to the ambush area (receiving from the surveillance helicopters up to date information on the situation), and take up concealed fire positions. Once there, the fire team leader and the Lynx aircrews are briefed on the positions of the leading enemy tanks. The fire team leader allocates the targets and directs the missile attacks of his team. Each Lynx rises vertically, exposing only the periscope sight on the roof of the cockpit above its cover, fires the missile, and keeps the sight trained on the target for the time needed by the TOW missile to reach the target (15 sec for 3,000m) and then drops down again. Used in this way, it is almost impossible to detect helicopters from the longer ranges, even with modern aids.[18]

Russian tank columns usually have with them the unpleasantly effective ZSU-23-4 quadruple 23mm SP anti-aircraft weapon, which carries its own fire control radar. This would probably be a first target for the ambushing helicopters, before turning their attention to the unprotected tanks.

In addition to using armed helicopters against tanks, infantry missile teams which can be transported by helicopters are being developed. These should be valuable in supplementing the efforts of the armed helicopters to contain an armoured breakthrough, but would not be an acceptable alternative to them. Once the infantry teams have been put down they are immobile, whilst the armed helicopter could fire eight missiles from eight different positions over a mile apart in as many minutes.[19] Ground teams used in this way could probably not be recovered by helicopter and would have to find their own way back, after firing all their missiles. The German and French Armies have in service light heliportable cross-country vehicles for this purpose and similar vehicles are to be provided in the British Army.

Only brief mention has been made so far of the other two major roles of the helicopters: reconnaissance and observation. But these two activities provide the eyes of the Army, and their importance can hardly be over-emphasised; for information as to what the enemy is doing can be vital to the conduct of battle — particularly defensive battle. There is some considerable difference between the two: reconnaissance implies the carrying out of a specific task for which the pilot has been briefed, and about which he is expected to render a report on his return; whilst observation, or surveillance, requires a continuous watch on the enemy, which is exhausting to both men and machines.[20]

The equal importance of reconnaissance and utility helicopters is recognised in the organisation of the Army Air Corps. In each armoured division there is an Army Air Corps Regiment consisting of two squadrons, one of which is equipped with Lynx helicopters and the other with Gazelles; each squadron having twelve helicopters. In addition to these divisional AAC regiments, there is another of similar size directly under Corps HQ.[21]

The helicopter has made enormous strides during its brief life, and it would be a bold man who would venture to forecast its future. History may provide indications. Armed helicopters, in their functions on the battlefield, are as much light cavalry in their relation to the heavy cavalry role of the battle tanks, as were the lancers and hussars of the past to the horse and heavy dragoons. Dragoons originally had the much lighter role of mounted infantry, but during the years they became indistinguishable from the horse; and hence the need to found a new light cavalry which, at first styled light dragoons, developed into lancers and hussars, In turn

their horses, equipment, and functions became similar to those of the heavy cavalry, and the lack of a real light cavalry resulted in the mounted infantry of the Boer War. Machine guns drove the horse from the battlefield, and following the subsequent development through two world wars of heavy and light tanks to fulfil the two traditional roles, we now have Chieftains to undertake the first, and armoured vehicles of the Scorpion family and helicopters the second. Perhaps helicopters, too, will eventually become 'heavy cavalry'.

Below: **A patrol of The Royal Highland Fusiliers (Princess Margaret's Own Glasgow and Ayshire Regiment) being dropped into a jungle clearing by a Whirlwind helicopter of the Royal Air Force.** / *Crown Copyright*

Right: **A Scout helicopter armed with SS11 missiles.** / *Crown Copyright*

Bottom right: **Gazelle helicopters of the Army Air Corps at the Royal Review in Germany in 1977. The Royal Standard flies from the bonnet of the Queen's car.** / *Crown Copyright*

Top: A Gazelle helicopter of the Army Air Corps taking up an observation position. / *Westland Helicopters Ltd*

Above: A Gazelle, blending with the background, on a reconnaissance mission. / *Crown Copyright*

Right: A Gazelle helicopter of No 656 Squadron Army Air Corps flying over the floating village of Aberdeen on Hong Kong Island. / *Crown Copyright*

Above: An Army Air Corps Gazelle helicopter landing on the deck of the Royal Fleet Auxiliary Landing Ship Logistic *Sir Geraint* near Ulvik, Norway, during an exercise. / *Crown Copyright*

Left: A Lynx helicopter of the Army Air Corps flying over Salisbury Plain. / *Crown Copyright*

Above right: A Lynx helicopter fitted with TOW missiles. / *Westland Helicopters Ltd*

Right: A Lynx helicopter firing SURA rockets. / *Westland Helicopters Ltd*

Right: The Westland Wisp remotely piloted helicopter.
/ Westland Helicopters Ltd

Below left, inset: A Gazelle helicopter flying over AFV 432s during the Royal Review. In the background are armed Scout helicopters and two Gazelles.
/ Crown Copyright

Below: A flight of Lynx helicopters of the Army Air Corps. */ Crown Copyright*

11
Communications and Electronics

Radar communications, radar transmissions, and the various forms of electronic gear used in guided weapons and detection have so increased in use and importance on the modern battlefield, that the stage has been reached when superiority in equipment or practice in this field could well provide the margin by which victory is achieved.

Communications

Because of the advances made in radio it is now the prime means of communication on the battlefield. Line communications are very vulnerable, unless deeply buried cable is used, and even light field cable is not flexible enough for extended fronts and mobile warfare. That does not imply that lines have no place in modern war, for they retain the advantage of being immune to jamming and being difficult to intercept.

The communications provided by the Royal Signals between corps headquarters and the headquarters of its armoured divisions, and between the latter and the headquarters of their task forces, are conducted over the ultra high frequency (UHF) 'Bruin' Area Trunk communication System. For telephone conversations the system works in a very similar fashion to the Post Office trunk dialling network in the United Kingdom. To provide flexibility and alternative routing in the event of damage from enemy action, there are a number of automatic switching points known as communications centres, or commonly as 'comcentres' or even 'comcens'. Each of the headquarters concerned has its own trunk dialling telephone number, and is connected to one or more comcentres. The comcentres are themselves inter-connected, so that if one should have been put out of action, the equipment will automatically connect a call by an alternative route. Mobile subscribers, wishing to join Bruin, can be connected to it by a system known as Single Channel Access.

Bruin is to be replaced in the 1980s by an even more sophisticated system called 'Ptarmigan'. It works on much the same principle, but Ptarmigan has provision for 21 comcentres as compared with Bruin's 10, and transmits voice, telegraph, facsimile, and data. In addition it will have a much improved speech security system. All Ptarmigan equipment will be mounted in vehicles.[1]

Inside a task force very high frequency (VHF) radio is used, and all commanders, from that of the infantry section upwards, are equipped with the appropriate VHF voice radio sets. Normally each unit and formation has its own radio net, with all concerned on the same frequency, eg platoon net, company net, battle group net, and task force command net. The Royal Artillery have their own system with all the guns of a battery on the same net. A tank squadron, too, is normally all on one net, whilst a squadron commander has a second net for communication with other squadrons and reconnaissance vehicles. The radio sets for these nets belong mostly to the remarkable 'Clansman' family. The smallest is the UK/PRC 350, measuring 9in×5½in×3in, for the section commander level, with a range of 5km and access to 840 channels in the 36-57Mhz range. At company level there is the larger UK/PRC 351, 10in×8½in×3¼in, having 1,840 channels with 25Khz spacing between 30 and 70MHz, and a range of 8km. A larger version of

this is the UK/PRC 352 with dimensions 14in×9in×4in and the increased range of 15km.[2] There are indeed Clansman radios for almost every conceivable purpose. The UK/PRC 344 is a UHF manpack equipment designed primarily as a communications link between forward air controllers and close support strike aircraft. The UK/PRC 320 is a HF radio for the Royal Artillery, which can be supplied as a manpack, a vehicle 'clip on', or a permanent installation in a vehicle. There are, too, the UK/VRC 321 and 322 HF vehicle stations, each covering the astounding number of 280,000 channels in the HF band, with voice, morse, and teletype facilities.[3] The UK/VRC 353 is also a vehicle radio, but this is VHF with a range of over 50km and a whip aerial. As an example of the vast improvement which has been effected, the Larkspur family, which preceded Clansman, offered 12 channels in the VHF band: Clansman provides 2,400.[4]

The British I Corps in BAOR is, of course, only one of the four corps in the British-commanded Northern Army Group; the others being German, Belgian and Dutch. Communications between Northern Army Group (or Northag) and its corps is provided by the remarkable Northag Signal Group, commanded by a German colonel with a Royal Signals lieutenant-colonel as his deputy commander, and composed of a unit from each of the four nations concerned. Building cable lines from HQ Northag to each of the four corps is the job of the 1st (Netherlands) Signal Squadron. The 840th (German) Signal Battalion is responsible for the radio relay links, carrying voice and teleprinter, between Northag and corps. The 28th (British) Signal Regiment, Royal Signals, is responsible for operating. It has a 120-line switchboard, mounted in a Mercedes diesel truck; a mobile computer, TARE (telegraphic automatic relay equipment) which reads a message, selects the appropriate circuit, and transmits it; and a mobile tropospheric scatter link, which uses the troposphere to bend back to the earth and scatter a signal which carries 60 channels. The 13th (Belgian) Signal Company has a reserve high frequency radio system for use if any of the above systems fail, or for providing point to point links to connect the Army Group Commander with each of his corps if he should otherwise be out of touch. In wartime the Signal Support Group would be reinforced by the 35th Signal Regiment (Volunteers) from the United Kingdom.[5]

Battlefield Surveillance

Information of enemy movements, actions, and strengths, is of vital importance to any commander, particularly if he is on the defensive, and even more particularly if his forces are much inferior in strength to those of the enemy.

Information is obtained by such means as the interception of communications and electronic transmissions, reconnaissance on the ground and in the air, and the various equipments that can be used to detect, or aid in detecting, enemy presence and movement. Surveillance on the battlefield can be divided into three zones. The nearest is that immediately in front of our own positions, and is a task for the troops occupying those positions. Next is the area forward of that line from a depth of about a mile to about 10 miles and reconnaissance of this zone would probably be carried out by the armoured reconnaissance regiments and the Army Air Corps, and its surveillance by the former only. The furthest zone, a belt stretching from a depth of 10 miles to say one of 30 miles, reaching probably well behind the enemy lines, would be covered by RAF reconnaissance flights.

Surveillance embraces three main tasks: detection, which is the discovery that the enemy is present; recognition, or the establishment of the nature of the enemy's presence, eg men or vehicles; and identification, or the type of enemy presence, eg an infantry patrol or battle tanks. Surveillance aids range from binoculars to the most sophisticated electronic devices. An image intensifier intensifies the ambient light (ie the light around the area on which attention is focused) so that on a night that is not quite pitch dark it is possible to see objects that would otherwise be invisible. A thermal imager detects the infra-red rays emitted by any object within its view both by day and night, converting them into pictures which are shown on a screen. Most thermal imagers are held in the hand and can take very good pictures in complete darkness. The principal British thermal imager is made by Hawker Siddeley Dynamics.[6]

Radar in surveillance detects but does not recognise, and those used on the battlefield can only detect moving objects. However, radar operators can often tell, by the tone in their earphones, the number of objects detected and their speed and nature. The Army has two types of man-portable radar: the French Oliphant II, weighing 9kg, which can detect a man at 1,800m and a vehicle at 2,400m; and the British Prowler which weighs only $3\frac{1}{2}$kg, but has the same range as Oliphant. Both are intended for use at company or platoon level. The standard British surveillance radar is the ZB 298 which weighs 32.3kg and requires two men to carry it. It can detect men at 5,000m and vehicles at 10,000m, and their presence can be either shown visually or given audibly in the headphones.

Mortar locating radars detect a mortar shell in at least two positions in flight, and from these a computer works out the trajectory and, by projecting it back, obtains the position of the mortar. One of the most successful mortar locating radars is the British 'Cymbeline' which is in service with the Army.[7]

A seismic detector is a small piece of equipment which is used to detect the ground vibrations made by the passage of vehicles or troops. These vibrations cause an electrical signal to be transmitted along a wire to a display unit, which can be some miles away. A British system in use by the Army is called 'Tobias'. The sensors are very small, measuring $2in \times 1\frac{1}{2}in \times 1\frac{1}{2}in$, and are buried just below the surface of the ground. From the display unit four lines of field cable run to four groups of 20 sensors each, giving a coverage of about 2.4km.[8]

Infra-red (IR) sensors can detect vehicles if their engines are hotter than their surroundings and a man's rifle if the barrel is still warm from firing. IR detectors can be used to assist sentries; a beam, for instance, thrown across a path or road and interrupted by the passing of man or vehicle, will trigger a visual or aural alarm at a control centre. The British Army has such a detector in service named 'Iris'.[9]

Lasers

Perhaps one of the most remarkable equipments to appear on the modern battlefield is the Laser, or **L**ight **A**mplification by the **S**timulated **E**mission of **R**adiation. Lasers today are used primarily for ranging and target marking. For ranging, an inherently narrow beam of laser light is fired at the target and a receiver clock measures the time taken for reflected energy to return. By comparing this time with the speed of light a range is obtained. The laser rangefinder is extremely accurate and can improve on previous methods by 70%. For tanks, this means that the main armament hit capability is so enhanced that targets which would previously have been rejected can be engaged with confidence.

A laser ranger can also be used for target designation, and Ferranti Limited have produced a single unit for target designation and ranging. The former is of particular value in aiding close air support. Modern air defences make it a hazardous business for aircraft to seek a target; but with the target illuminated by a laser beam the task becomes infinitely easier. The aircraft is fitted with a laser seeker, and as it comes into view the forward air controller aims the laser designator at the target and switches on. The airborne laser seeker locks on and when a laser guided weapon is released it homes on to the energy scattered by the target.[10]

Laser can be made powerful enough to burn through armour at tactically useful ranges, but the generators required to power such weapons are too heavy and bulky at the moment to be of operational use.[11] Nevertheless, we are within sight of the 'death ray' of science-fiction.

Electronic Warfare

Having regard to the prime importance on the modern battlefield of radio communications, radar, laser, and electronically guided missiles, it is apparent that jamming and preventing jamming are the major considerations in what has been termed electronic warfare (EW). It includes:

a Electronic Intelligence (ELINT), or the acquisition of information regarding the enemy's weapon systems and sensors
b Electronic Support Measures (ESM), which means receiving and analysing enemy electronic transmissions in order to select the appropriate counter-action
c Electronic Counter-Measures (ECM), which are those taken to counter enemy activity, eg jamming
d Electronic Counter-Counter-Measures, or the steps taken to nullify the hostile ECM

Soviet tanks are known to rely heavily on radio communications, and having regard to the rigid Russian tactical doctrines and the restricted initiative allowed to junior commanders, the successful jamming of those communications might throw a whole plan of attack out of gear. Most of these communications, however, are VHF or UHF, with line of sight paths, so that a jammer would have to be close to their receivers or airborne above them, eg a Remote Piloted Vehicle (RPV).

In the Navy and Air Force most EW equipment is designed to counter missiles which home on to ships or aircraft. The Army does not at present have to counter many such missiles, because most of those used in land warfare are either guided by wires or else steer themselves by inertial navigation. But, missiles, and later probably shells, guided by laser reflections from the target pose a new problem; and to these will

Below: **A section radio operator of The King's Own Royal Border Regiment; Private A. Harvey of the Chindit Company.** / *Museum of The King's Own Royal Border Regiment*

soon be added missiles able to home themselves by television or by receiving natural infra-red emissions from the target. The American anti-tank 'Hellfire' is under development, and the Anglo-French 'Martel' will be able to home either by television (British version) or by receiving the target's radar emission (French version). Many missiles which home on to a target only switch on their radars a few seconds before hitting it, and in those few seconds the inteceptor has to receive the missile's transmission, identify it, and switch on his jammer or other device.[12]

ECM against radar includes detecting, fixing, monitoring, jamming, and deceiving enemy radars. Hand-held miniature radar warning receivers will give an indication when they are receiving radar signals. The direction of such a radar transmission can then be found by turning the receiver till the signal is at its greatest strength. This will give the approximate direction of an enemy position and enable a patrol, for instance, to avoid it. The British HWR2 hand-held receiver is on issue to the Army. An enemy battlefield radar can be jammed, but this has the disadvantage that the enemy could get a bearing on the jamming transmitter.[13]

ECCM can be built into a weapon system, and modern radars incorporate a 'frequency agility' system for this purpose. This is a means of varying the radiated frequency very rapidly and in an entirely random way, so that an enemy jammer has great difficulty in following the frequency changes. It has proved very effective and is being incorporated in all new weapon systems which rely on radar.[14]

Lasers present a particular ECM problem, especially as at present a target does not know that it is being illuminated by a laser. In the USA laser countermeasures are being developed. One of these, the **La**ser **Ho**ming **a**nd **W**arning **S**ystem (LAHAWS) informs the personnel at the target that they are being illuminated and gives the direction of the hostile laser designator, which is pointed at the target by the operator. A much more powerful defensive laser is then directed at the enemy operator, destroying his eye and making useless the optics of his sight. If this is done in time the enemy laser beam would wander and the missile that it was directing would fail to lock on to the target.[15]

Left: A manpack HF radio set, the PRC 351 for infantry battalions.
/ *RHQ Royal Signals*

Below: The HF radio set D13 of 14 Signal Regiment, Royal Signals; used for long distance communications between major formations.
/ *RHQ Royal Signals*

Right: An underground cable layer for airfield communications.
/ *RHQ Royal Signals*

Below right: A radio detachment Royal Signals, on an exercise in Norway.
/ *RHQ Royal Signals*

Above: Guiding three-pair underground cable into a trench.
/ *RHQ Royal Signals*

Right: Royal Artillery meteorological system (AMETS) radar.
/ *Crown Copyright*

Above: FV102 Striker, a member of the CVR(T) Scorpion family, firing a Swingfire anti-tank wire-guided missile. The wire from an earlier firing can be seen trailing from the launch container. / *MoD*

Below: The British Army's M2 self-propelled bridge unit can be used solo as a ferry or in multiple to form a floating bridge. Here it is carrying an FV432. / *COI*

Two pictures that span the broad spectrum of activities of the modern soldier. *Above:* The Guards Trooping the Colour in front of the Old Admiralty Building on Horseguards' Parade. *Below:* An FV434 fitter's vehicle servicing a Chieftain MBT while in the background five other Chieftains and their crews bivouac. / *MoD; Robin Adshead*

Above: **The Army Air Corps' second Lynx AH-1 helicopter on trials carrying eight TOW anti-tank missiles.** / *Westland Helicopters*

Below: **Men in full NBC dress firing an 81mm mortar; note Sterling SMGs on pit rim.** / *MoD*

Right: Stalwart high mobility load carrier crossing a river. The FV622 Stalwart is really three vehicles in one, providing conventional road, cross-country and amphibious transport for up to 5,000kg of cargo. In the latter mode Stalwart can achieve over five knots in open sea. / *COI*

Below: A patrol of camouflaged infantrymen all armed with the standard FN 7.62mm rifle. Soldier in foreground is carrying radio manpack with boom microphone. / *MoD*

12

Other Equipments

It is not proposed in this chapter to deal with all the other equipments of the Army but only those of particular interest.

Bridging

The bridging of waterways is of major importance for a mobile and mechanised army, and speed in the erection of bridges may well spell the difference between success and failure. The Royal Engineers have a number of different types of bridge to suit different conditions and different obstacles. Of these, the Medium Girder Bridge has been claimed as the most advanced and versatile army bridging system in the western world. It was developed by the Military Vehicles and Engineering Establishment of the Ministry of Defence and is manufactured by Fairey Engineering. By the use of specially developed aluminium alloy and novel methods of assembly, a great saving has been achieved in the time and effort needed to build bridges in the battle area. The Medium Girder Bridge, or MGB, can be assembled as either a single or a double storey construction of varying lengths. It will carry Class 60 loads in single span over gaps of up to 30.5m (100ft), or, with a Reinforcement Kit, 49m. With Span Junction Sets, multispan bridging can be erected on either existing or improvised piers; or with MGB Portable Pier Sets, floating bridges can be produced in double or single form. There are only seven components, but with these many bridge variations can be constructed. The basic unit is a light alloy box section top panel 1.8m (6ft) in length. Sections can be rapidly joined together to make a pair of long girders which form the load carrying members of the bridge. A light alloy decking is then laid between them to give a road-way four metres (13ft 2in) wide. For long spans and heavy loads the side girders can be deepened by the addition of triangular bottom panels. Ramp units are placed directly on the ground at each end of the bridge to give access to it. The bridge can be assembled in 1.8m increments by a NCO and 24 men, and a 30.5m single span Class 60 bridge takes less than an hour.[1]

Another type of bridge is the lightweight Class 16, which can be assembled as a clearspan bridge, a floating bridge, or a powered raft. The basic components are deck boxes, ramps, articulator boxes, floats, and sponsons. The deck box combines the functions of bridge girders and cross girders, and contributes buoyancy to the floating bridge and the raft. The top of the box forms the deck of the bridge. A 15.2m (50ft) clearspan bridge is assembled from seven deck boxes and two pairs of ramps by 16 men in about 20min. A floating bridge 58m (192ft) long can be built from 40 deck boxes, two pairs of articulator boxes (fixed between deck boxes and ramps to allow adjustment for bank heights), two pairs of ramps, and floats. There is no limit, however, to the length of floating bridge that can be constructed. Components can be moved in special trailers or carried by transport aircraft or helicopters.[2]

Portable Roadways

Areas of mud, marsh, sand, and other difficult going can present hazards for vehicles. In World War II the expanded metal, or XPM, road was produced for such conditions, but this has now been superseded by the Class 30 and Class 60 Trackways, which are much easier to handle and can be laid much more quickly. Furthermore, they are easily transported and can be rapidly recovered for use elsewhere. The Class 30 trackway is designed for wheeled vehicles and for tracked vehicles with rubber pads. It can be launched and recovered by standard transport vehicles. It is assembled from a number of extruded aluminium alloy planks with interlocking joints, and one length is usually 50m. It is normally carried on a spool, mounted on a heavy truck, and from this the 50m can be laid over soft ground in about one minute, following some nine minutes preparation. The spool is carried on a frame and turntable assembly, clamped to the truck platform, and the trackway is launched forward over the truck cab. It is recovered over the rear of the truck. The trackway can also be laid from a roll suspended from a helicopter.

The Class 60 heavy duty trackway is designed for both tracked and wheeled vehicles. It is generally used to support battle tanks over very soft ground and in areas where there are large concentrations of vehicles on a spongy surface. It is made of a heavier aluminium plank and can be laid either from a made up roll or by sliding individual planks together on the ground.[3]

The Combat Engineer Tractor

A very useful Royal Engineer vehicle is the FV 180 Combat Engineer Tractor, which is both armoured and amphibious, and has the distinction of being the only purpose-built machine of its kind in any army. It is built by the Royal Ordnance Factory, Leeds, and its facilities include two powerful rear-mounted water jets to enable it to swim rivers, and a rocket-fired anchor and hawser to winch itself out of boggy ground. It operates as a bulldozer or digger, and can be fitted with a crane, an 8ton winch, and a fender for landing pontoons, and it can carry a pre-fabricated trackway which unrolls ahead of it when crossing soft surfaces. It can also tow trailers and construction plant and operate certain ancillary equipment. Apart from swimming, it can wade and work in shallow water. Its maximum speed is 40mph.[4]

RCT Equipment

The Royal Corps of Transport has such a wide range of vehicles and other equipment, that to describe even all the most interesting would take far more space than this chapter can allow. One of its most impressive looking vehicles is the six-wheeled Stalwart amphibious carrier, with a speed on the road of 39mph and through the water of 6.2mph. It is driven through the latter by two mechanically activated water propulsion units, and steered by hinged cowls. It can carry a load of about five tons.

The Eager Beaver fork lift tractor has been designed specifically to handle military loads in difficult terrain, including soft sand, deep mud and all uneven surfaces. It can carry 4,000lb and has a top speed of over 40mph. The forks are mounted on a mast assembly which is hydraulically operated for elevation, tilt and traverse movement. Partially stripped, it can be carried in transport aircraft.[5]

A somewhat similar, but more ambitious vehicle, is the Liner

Company's Giraffe. Unlike a conventional fork lift, the Giraffe has no fork mast, and the fork carriage is mounted on a pivoted telescopic boom. Loads can not only be lifted, but they can also be projected forward, and the Giraffe can load and unload vehicles from one side and place loads over obstructions.[6]

Another lifting equipment is the Modular Distribution System, a portable gear for removing containers from trucks. It is capable of lifting a Scorpion tank, weighing over seven tons.[7]

One of the most useful equipments to appear recently is the Ampliroll. It is manufactured by Hearncrest Boughton Engineering and is a mechanical and hydraulic apparatus which can be fitted on to a standard vehicle chassis for loading and lifting. Mounted on a Foden 8 × 4 flat rack lorry, an Ampliroll can exchange its cargoes or swap bodies in approximately three minutes. The operation is carried out by the driver alone and unaided from the driving seat.[8] In a light recovery role it can load on any of the Scorpion range of tracked vehicles. The Royal Corps of Transport now have various equipments for this 'Swap Body System', including 3,500gal tanker bodies, 18cu yd tippers, and containers.[9] Ampliroll is one of the most useful aids to the rapid loading, unloading, and turn-round of vehicles.

Arctic warfare demands special vehicles, and the RCT has the 'Carrier, Full Tracked Articulated' for transporting personnel and material across snow covered country. This consists of two units with wide rubber tracks, connected by Universal couplings. The front car accommodates the crew and contains the Volvo engine, gearboxes, and steering assembly, whilst the rear car can carry eight men or the equivalent weight of material. Alternative roles include the carriage of the Wombat, lifting the 81mm mortar, REME recovery, the carriage of REME fitters, a command vehicle, and an ambulance.[10] There are other vehicles, too, for operating in these conditions, including the Norwegian Army type Volvo Weasels.

Of general purpose vehicles, the admirable Landrover is of special note because of its many manifestations. The Rover General Service half-tonne truck can be carried by transport aircraft or lifted by helicopter, can carry a useful payload, and is capable of towing light support weapons. There is also a special radio equipped version. There is a heavier three-quarter tonne truck which is based on the commercial Landrover, and this also can be used as a general carrier or be specially fitted for radio. Finally, Rover produce a one-tonne General Service truck as a helicopter liftable load carrier. A most useful maid of all work is the Bedford four-wheeled 4-tonne truck with four wheel drive. Bedford trucks (or lorries, as they used to be called) have been load carriers for the Army for very many years. For really heavy loads there is the Leyland 10-tonne truck with all its six wheels driven. It is designed to facilitate side and end loading with mechanical aids. An identical chassis and winch are used for the tractor which tows medium artillery.[11]

Tank transportation is an important RCT responsibility; that is, the lifting of tanks to save the wear on their tracks. An operation involving tanks and their transporters was vividly described recently in *Soldier* magazine as follows:

'With an ear-shattering roar, 32 Antar tank transporters and 32 Chieftains passed in quick succession through the filter point — each tank following its parent mover. The scene was a demonstration by 16 Tank Transporter Squadron, Royal Corps of Transport, on Hohne Ranges in Germany . . . At a given signal, 32 Chieftains of 4th/7th Royal Dragoon Guards raced from their hides in the surrounding woods to link up with the almost two-kilometre-long convoy of transporters on the range road . . . As each 52 ton battle tank left the range it drove into the convoy immediately behind its transporter before being driven on to the trailer.'[12]

The Thornycroft Antar is a heavy 6 × 6 tractor which tows a multi-wheel trailer ten metres long.

The Royal Corps of Transport has a Maritime Detachment which operates a fleet of support ships and boats. The pride of the fleet are the two recently commissioned Landing Craft Logistic (LCL) *Ardennes* and *Arakan* each of 1,500 tons. When Her Majesty's Army Vessel *Ardennes* was commissioned in December 1977 she was described as 'the largest and most expensive bit of kit the Army has ever owned'. HMAV *Arakan* was commissioned in the summer of 1978. Both ships have a speed of ten knots and a range of 4,000 miles. They are each commanded by a major with a crew of 35 officers and soldiers. They run weekly container cargoes from Marchwood Military Port to Antwerp with goods and vehicles for the Rhine Army, and they also carry general cargo to the Royal Artillery ranges in the Outer Hebrides.[13]

Recovery

The vital importance of recovery, particularly of tanks, was discussed in Chapter 7. The Royal Electrical and Mechanical Engineers have a number of different types of recovery vehicle in service. There are Armoured Recovery Vehicles based on the Chieftain and Centurion tanks and there is also the Samson in the Scorpion series of tracked armoured vehicles. REME also have the AFV 434 with the Light Aid Detachments for the recovery and first line repair of vehicles in the battle groups of BAOR. Prominent amongst non-armoured recovery vehicles is AEC 6 × 6, which can recover all wheeled vehicles up to and including the 10-tonne class, and the Leyland recovery vehicle with a low loader trailer, used by LADs in armoured regiments and mechanised

Below: A class 40 Single Storey Medium Girder Bridge, constructed by the Royal Engineers. / *Crown Copyright*

Right: Soldiers of 68 Gurkha Field Squadron of The Queen's Gurkha Engineers laying decking pieces on a double Storey Medium Girder Bridge in Hong Kong. / *Crown Copyright*

Below right: A Scorpion of C Squadron (medium reconnaissance) 16th/5th The Queen's Royal Lancers on a double storey Class 60 medium girder bridge, built by the 68th Gurkha Field Squadron in Hong Kong. / *Crown Copyright*

infantry battalions in BAOR. By attaching a 'Dummy Axle Trailer' behind it, a standard army truck can be used for recovering a casualty vehicle requiring a suspended tow.[14]

Protective Clothing

Protective clothing is not one of the more glamorous types of army equipment, yet it is essential if the soldier is to be protected against the nasty hazards which are collectively known as NCB ie nuclear fall-out, chemical (that is, various forms of gas) attack, or biological warfare (typically, the use of germs to spread disease). Protection from all of these is provided by the service respirator, disposable smock and trousers, and gauntlets. Wearing such clothing is a great handicap to activity, so that it is obvious that an enemy who uses NCB weapons must be compelled to wear it for fear of retaliation.[15]

Left: A Chieftain main battle tank on a double storey medium girder bridge. / *Crown Copyright*

Right: British forces crossing the Rhine on a raft belonging to the Federal Republic of Germany. / *Crown Copyright*

Below: A Chieftain crossing an M2 bridge over the River Weser. The M2 is an amphibious bridge system, of German design, consisting of decked vehicles driven into the water and connected together. / *Crown Copyright*

BRIDGE
STARTS

Left: Sappers of the Royal Engineers erecting an M2 bridge over the River Weser in Germany. / *Crown Copyright*

Below left: M2 bridge building across the Weser note the bridge vehicles side by side. / *Crown Copyright*

Right: Another view of M2 bridge construction. / *Crown Copyright*

Below: Chieftain tanks crossing the completed M2 bridge over the River Weser. / *Crown Copyright*

Above: Brigadier A. Dennis, Commander 20th Armoured Brigade, thumbing a lift on a Chieftain tank of The Blues and Royals (Royal Horse Guards and 1st Dragoons), which has just crossed the River Weser M2 bridge. / *Crown Copyright*

Left: A heavy girder bridge being constructed in 1969 at Caernarvon Castle for the investiture of the Prince of Wales by 32 Field Squadron of the 38th Engineer Regiment, Royal Engineers. / *Crown Copyright*

Above right: Royal Engineers erecting a Bailey Bridge over the River Ouse. / *Crown Copyright*

Right: A Class 30 Trackway Dispenser and track belonging to 43 Field Support Squadron, Royal Engineers in West Germany. / *Crown Copyright*

Above left: **A Combat Engineer Tractor towing the Giant Viper anti-tank mine clearing equipment.** / *Crown Copyright*

Left: **A Combat Engineer Tractor entering the water.** / *Crown Copyright*

Above: **A Combat Engineer Tractor swimming.** / *Crown Copyright*

Right: **A Stalwart amphibious carrier of the Royal Corps of Transport emerging from a German river.** / *Crown Copyright*

116

Left: A Royal Corps of Transport Stalwart crossing a German river. / *Crown Copyright*

Below left: A Stalwart moving across rough country. / *Crown Copyright*

Right: An Eager Beaver fork lift truck of the Royal Corps of Transport. / *Crown Copyright*

Below: An Eager Beaver, showing steering. / *Crown Copyright*

Left: A Liner Giraffe telescopic handler. / *Crown Copyright*

Below: The Modular Distribution System. / *Crown Copyright*

Right: Ampliroll: loading a Scorpion light tank. / *Crown Copyright*

Below right: Ampliroll with Spartan loaded. / *Crown Copyright*

Left: Tanker body for Ampliroll, holding 3,500gal. / *Crown Copyright*

Below left: Craftsman John Kurzera of 9 Field Workshop Royal Electrical and Mechanical Engineers repairing the engine of a Volvo tracked articulated carrier. / *Crown Copyright*

Right: The articulated carrier on the move during exercises in Norway. / *Crown Copyright*

Below: Norwegian Army Volvo Weasels with 106mm anti-tank guns, after disembarking from a SRN 6 Mark V hovercraft during an exercise in Norway by the Hovercraft Trials Squadron of the Royal Corps of Transport. / *Crown Copyright*

Top left: A Volvo articulated tracked carrier of the 1st Battalion The Royal Anglian Regiment during an exercise in Norway.

Above: A Land Rover in tough going. / *Crown Copyright*

Left: A Snow-Trac towing skiers; a method of travel that is called 'Ski-Joring'. / *Crown Copyright*

Left: A Ramped Powered Lighter of the Royal Corps of Transport; used mainly for heavy lighterage. / Crown Copyright

Below left: A Centurion based armoured recovery vehicle of The Royal Hussars (Prince of Wale's Own) pulling a Chieftain tank out of its trouble. / Crown Copyright

Right: AFV 434 Light Aid Detachment Repair and Recovery Vehicle of the Royal Electrical and Mechanical Engineers for first line repairs within battle groups. / Crown Copyright

Below: A Leyland recovery vehicle towing a low load trailer. / Crown Copyright

Organisation and Functions

13

The Regular and Reserve Armies

The organisation and tasks of the Army are described in the Defence White Paper of 1978 (the latest available at the time of writing). At the beginning of the paper the policy on which organisation and tasks are based is stated as follows:

'United Kingdom Defence Policy is based on the North Atlantic Alliance... The Government policy continues to concentrate our defence effort on the Alliance in the ways that can best contribute to the strength of the Alliance and thus to our own security.'

It is this political intention that governs to a great extent the distribution and higher organisation of our fighting Services. The Paper implies that our armed forces must be strong, because it goes on to say: 'A major defence effort... is indeed a precondition of successful political action. We must therefore continue to make a proper contribution to NATO's strategy of deterrence.' It continues:

'That strategy is based on forward defence and the capability of flexible response. Forward defence means that NATO is committed to defend the full territorial integrity of its members and to halt any attack at the earliest possible point. Flexible response means that NATO must have a range of military options wide enough to ensure that whatever form aggression took NATO would have the ability to meet it effectively without having to face an intolerable choice between conceding defeat and using dangerously excessive force from the start. For this purpose NATO deploys three main levels of forces — conventional, theatre nuclear, and strategic nuclear. The three levels are inter-dependent and successful defence requires a balanced combination of them... Theatre nuclear weapons are needed to deter the use of similar weapons by the Soviet Union... The use of nuclear weapons would be a matter for the closest political control, but the knowledge that they will be used if necessary to stop aggression is an essential element in deterrence. Finally, without a strong conventional capability the Alliance would be bound to rely heavily on nuclear weapons...'

This statement does not perhaps bear very close examination. The possession of theatre nuclear weapons to stop the Russians using them is a valid reason, and the same argument could be extended to the possession of chemical weapons. The insistence on a strong conventional capability is also sound, but there is a suggestion that because it is not strong enough nuclear weapons might have to be used; although, because of their close political control, agreement by some nine Governments might take time — unless the Russians used them first! In any case, there is some doubt as to whether it would be practicable to use them at all. The Defence White Paper does not appear to be too optimistic about NATO's ability to defeat with conventional weapons a conventional Soviet attack. In Central Europe it says that the Warsaw Pact forces have about two and a half times NATO's strength in main battle tanks, artillery, and tactical aircraft. And even this does not complete the depressing disparity, because of 'the state of readiness of Warsaw Pact forces in Europe, which has always exceeded that of the NATO forces and has recently been improved, and the continued

introduction of new equipment.' There is another Warsaw Pact advantage which the White Paper does not mention. Because in any war they would be the aggressors, they would have the initiative at the opening of hostilities, with the capability of concentrating swiftly and without warning at their chosen points of attack on the very wide front. This, it has been calculated, could enable them to achieve a local superiority as high as 20 or 30 to one in each of four or five separate thrusts.[1] The aim of such thrusts would be to break right through the NATO defences in rapid armoured drives across the territory of the German Federal Republic to reach the Rhine.

The major part of the British Army is committed to NATO, but it also, of course, has to fulfil various national tasks as well. The strongest British force overseas is the British Army of the Rhine, which contributes the First British Corps to NATO's Northern Army Group (NORTHAG). This, together with the Central Army Group (CENTAG) on its right, constitutes the land part of Allied Forces Central Europe (AFCENT). The peacetime establishment of BAOR is 55,000 men, which, says the White Paper, can be doubled in an emergency. Its equipment includes over 600 Chieftain tanks, and over 2,000 other armoured fighting vehicles. The Army also provides troops for the Strategic Reserve of the Supreme Allied Commander Europe (SACEUR). These consist of the Allied Mobile Force (AMF) of some 4,000 men which is intended for rapid deployment on the flanks of Allied Command Europe (ACE), and the general reserve which can be employed anywhere in ACE. The British element of the latter is the United Kingdom Mobile Force (UKMF).

In addition to these NATO forces, the Army's tasks include the land defence of the United Kingdom, the provision of overseas garrisons, security operations in Northern Ireland and elsewhere, contributions to United Nations peace keeping forces, and the maintenance of troops for any contingencies that may arise. In time of war, however, it is planned that some 70% of the Regular and Reserve Army will be deployed to the European mainland and that most of the remainder will remain to defend the United Kingdom.

In order to fulfill these commitments the British Army in peacetime is organised as follows:

a The First British Corps of four armoured divisions, an artillery division, and the 5th Field Force less certain elements. (A field force has no fixed formation, but a typical allotment of units would consist of: three infantry battalions; an artillery field regiment; a guided weapon battery; an armoured reconnaissance regiment; a signal squadron; an engineer regiment, less one squadron; a squadron of the Army Air Corps; a transport squadron; an ordnance company; a field workshop; a field ambulance; and a provost company. It is thus a force of all arms, capable of operating independently.)
b The Berlin Field Force, about 3,000 strong, which is not assigned to NATO and which is the British contribution to the security of West Berlin.
c The United Kingdom Land Forces (UKLF) which include the 6th, 7th, and 8th Field Forces. The 6th Field Force and the Logistic Support Group form the land component of the UKMF. The 7th Field Force

forms part of the reinforcements that bring BAOR up to its war establishment; and the 8th Field Force has responsibilities in connection with the defence of the United Kingdom. The British contingent in the AMF consists of an infantry battalion, force artillery headquarters, an artillery battery, a reconnaissance squadron, a radio troop, half of the force helicopter unit, an air support centre, an intelligence detachment, and the Logistic Support Battalion.[2]

Altogether the field units of the Regular Army include 10 armoured regiments, nine armoured reconnaissance regiments, 22 artillery regiments of various types, 10 engineer regiments, and 55 infantry battalions (of which five are Gurkha).

The Reserves

Apart from these Regular units, the White Paper shows the important part played by the TAVR in bringing the Army up to its post-mobilisation strength, for it lists two armoured reconnaissance regiments, five artillery regiments, seven engineer regiments, 11 signal regiments, 38 battalions of infantry, two Special Air Service regiments, one regiment of the Honourable Artillery Company, eight transport regiments, as well as light aid detachments, ordnance field parks, etc.

There are two principal categories of reserves. The first of these is composed of officers and soldiers who have completed their service with the Regular Army, but who have a compulsory liability for reserve service, and who can be recalled to the Colours in an emergency. The Regular Army Reserve of Officers consists of officers transferred into it from the Regular Army, but also from the TAVR. Their average age and seniority tends to be high, but comparatively few of them are required on mobilisation, so that there is ample scope for selection.

Soldiers of the Regular Army who leave the Colours before completing 12 years service are liable to serve in the Regular Reserve. Normally, Colour and Reserve service together will not exceed 12 years, so that a soldier who completes 12 years with the Colours has no liability to serve in the Regular Reserve, though he could volunteer for Section D. After completion of Colour and Regular Reserve service men are transferred to the Long Term Reserve, where they remain till the age of 45. (This does not apply to those who become Service pensioners after 22 years Colour service.) Regular reservists are liable for annual training but this obligation is not at present invoked.

The regular Reserve is divided into three Sections: A, B, and D. Section A is composed of men who have left the Colours with less than 12 years service and are subject to recall by the Secretary of State for Defence when warlike operations are in preparation or in progress, in addition to the liabilities of Section B. In Section B are those men who have a period of reserve service to complete but who for some reason cannot be placed in Section A. They may be called up for service at home or overseas by a Queen's Order when national danger is imminent or a great emergency has arisen, and by the Secretary of State for the defence of the United Kingdom against actual or apprehended attack.

Soldiers who have completed their service in Sections A or B, and who wish to continue in the Regular Reserve, may do so by re-engaging in Section D, provided they are fit and needed. They may opt for either Section A or Section B recall liability.

Reservists are transferred to the Long Term Reserve (LTR) when they have completed their Colour and Regular Reserve service. The LTR may be called up under the same terms as Section B. Pensioners (those who have completed 22 years Colour service) are also liable to recall under the same terms as Section B, but they must be given three days warning.[3]

The second type of reserve force is the Territorial and Army Volunteer Reserve (TAVR). It was formed on 1 April 1967 from the Territorial Army and the Army Emergency Reserve (formerly the Supplementary Reserve). Its cumbersome title is derived from the first words of the titles of its components, with the addition of 'Volunteer', which itself was the title of the force from which the Territorials were formed in 1908. In practice the 'and' is increasingly dropped, so that it becomes 'Territorial Army Volunteer Reserve', which sounds a great deal better. As so many of its units are described as 'Volunteer', an even better title would be 'Volunteer Reserve'.

The Territorial Army was formed as a self-contained force for home defence, consisting of some 14 divisions and other troops. In World War I most Territorials volunteered for overseas service and a large number of divisions fought on the Western front and elsewhere. After World War I overseas service in time of war became part of the obligation, but it was intended that units should have six months training after mobilisation. It will be remembered from Chapter 5 that, owing to deficiencies in the Regular Army order of battle, some Territorial units

had to go overseas with the British Expeditionary Force immediately after mobilisation. But it did demonstrate that the enthusiasm of the part-time soldier enabled him to become efficient far more quickly than the average conscript.

The Army Emergency Reserve consisted of specialist units of various arms which were needed to support both the Regular Army and the Territorial Army. The AER recruited men whose civilian trades gave them specialist skills which could not be taught in the time available to the Territorial.

The TAVR is not, like the Territorial Army, a separate force with its own divisions and order of battle. It supplies units and individuals to reinforce the Regular Army formations committed to NATO, and those earmarked for the defence of the United Kingdom, and it is also required to provide communications and other assistance to the civil authority in the United Kingdom, if the need should arise in time of war. Its units are required, too, to go into action immediately on the outbreak of war, without any post-mobilisation training. This of course implies an extremely high standard of instruction and elite permanent staffs.

The TAVR comprises Independent Units and Sponsored Units. The former provide by far the greater majority (about 82%) and are the descendants of the regiments and corps of the Territorial Army. They recruit locally and have their own permanent staff and premises (TAVR Centres), where they keep most of their equipment. On mobilisation they collect the balance of their equipment and supplies from Ordnance Depots in the United Kingdom, and those with an overseas role move to BAOR and elsewhere. Equipment which is awkward to move across the Channel is pre-stocked in BAOR Ordnance Depots.[4]

Sponsored units, like their AER predecessors, are mainly technical and specialist, and they are recruited throughout the whole country, rather than in one country or town. They do not, for that reason, have their own TAVR Centres, and they are sponsored by a Central Volunteer headquarters of their own arm or service.[5]

The TAVR establishment (1978) is 5,900 officers and 67,000 soldiers, and its strength at the time of writing is about 60,000 all ranks. From this it provides about 25% of the mobilisation order of battle.[6] All members of the TAVR have an annual training obligation. For Independent units this consists of 15 days in camp, 12 days out-of-camp training, and 13 days of such voluntary training as their commanding officer may decide. Units which have an overseas role in time of war, do their camp training period in the theatre to which they are allocated Sponsored units do the same period of training in camp, but their out of camp training is limited to four days and there is no voluntary training. As they only need the basic military training, this lesser obligation suffices.[7]

A defect of the Regular Reserve in 1939 was that many of the men recalled to the Colours were unfamiliar with the new equipment that had been received by the Army since their Colour service had expired; eg 25-pounder guns and Bren light machine guns. Fortunately there was plenty of time for the necessary individual training. In order to avoid this happening again, and also to maintain standards of efficiency, it would appear advisable to invoke the training obligation for Regular reservists. The importance of this is shown by the size of the Regular Reserve; the strength of which, according to the White Paper, is 116,000, in all its categories of the Regular Army Reserve of Officers, the Regular Reserve, the LTR, and the Army Pensioners. Serving with the Colours, by comparison, there are 17,000 officers and 139,000 soldiers.

The TAVR is probably potentially a great deal stronger than the figures suggest, because every year there is a turnover of between a quarter and a third of a unit's strength through men leaving for various reasons and others being recruited in their place.[8] In time of war many of the former would probably wish to re-enlist.

Top right: A general view of the Royal Review of the Army in Germany in 1977. Some 4,000 soldiers and 550 armoured vehicles took part: the largest parade of armour ever held by the British Army. / *Crown Copyright*

Centre right: 1st Divisional Headquarters and Signal Regiment, Royal Signals, on parade. / *RHQ Royal Signals*

Right: Soldiers of the 1st Battalion The Parachute Regiment leaving their parachutes in the dropping zone and making for the rendezvous. / *Film Company Photographs*

Top: Gunners of 148 (Meiktila) Commando Forward Observation Battery, Royal Artillery, whose role is to support the Royal Marines and other NATO troops by directing naval gunfire and air strikes on to enemy targets during an amphibious assault. In their fast inflatable Gemini boats, they would be amongst the first men ashore. / *Crown Copyright*

Above: Briefing, with the aid of an improvised map in a jungle training camp in Belize. / *Crown Copyright*

Left: Soldiers of the 1st Battalion The Staffordshire Regiment (The Prince of Wales's) on a jungle patrol in Belize. / *Crown Copyright*

Top right: Army Assault craft during training in The Gambia, West Africa. / *Crown Copyright*

Right: Soldiers of the TAVR on an exercise to test the speed with which they could reinforce NATO. / *Crown Copyright*

14

The Armoured Division

An examination of the organisation of the new pattern British Armoured Division should give a general idea of how all arms of the Service fit in and work together in the British Army of today.

During the last few years there has been a radical reorganisation of the Army's fighting formations — a reorganisation that was carried out as a result of the Defence Review of 1974. In brief, the brigade as an echelon of command between a divisional headquarters and its units was abolished, and the armoured division, now the only type of division, was made much smaller.

The right balance of arms in an armoured division and their tactical organisation has always presented a problem. Improvements in tanks and anti-tank weapons have led to alterations in tactics and consequent amendments to the proportions of units and equipments.

The Armoured Division of 1939, the first of its kind in the British Army, consisted of a Light Armoured Brigade (three light tank regiments equipped with cruiser tanks and light tanks), a Heavy Armoured Brigade (three heavy regiments with cruiser tanks only) and a Support Group (a motorised rifle battalion, a motorised artillery regiment, and an engineer company). The ratio of armour to infantry was therefore six to one. Early in 1940 a second infantry battalion and an anti-tank/anti-aircraft regiment were added to the support group and the two armoured brigades were made similar, each with three regiments equipped with cruiser tanks. As a result of the 1940 campaign in France and Flanders, an armoured car regiment was added for reconnaissance, and the combined anti-tank/anti-aircraft regiment was split to provide separate regiments for each role. At the same time the second infantry battalion in the support group was removed, but an infantry battalion was included in each armoured brigade; so that the ratio of armour to infantry was now two to one.

In the German Army, in the meantime, the victories in the West were followed by a doubling of the number of armoured divisions; but there were insufficient tanks to provide two regiments (ie six battalions) in each division. The number of tank regiments in a division was therefore reduced to one, and, furthermore, while in six divisions the regiment had three battalions, in the remaining divisions there were only two. The new pattern battalion had two light companies with Pz III 50mm gun tanks and one medium company with Pz IV 75mm gun tanks, whilst Pz II 20mm gun tanks were retained for reconnaissance. The infantry brigade of the armoured division was reorganised to comprise two two-battalion motorised rifle regiments and one motorcycle rifle battalion. There were three artillery battalions and one anti-aircraft regiment with 88mm guns (which were later to become all too effective in an anti-tank role!). In the smaller armoured division, therefore, the ratio of armour to infantry was only two to five.

As a result of experience in the Western Desert, and before the battle of El Alamein in October 1942, a new organisation was introduced for a British armoured division which was very similar to the German. The latter had come about through a shortage of tanks, but German experience had shown it to be an admirably balanced fighting force. The new British division had one armoured brigade of three armoured regiments and one infantry battalion, and a motorised infantry brigade of three battalions. The support group was removed and the artillery was increased to two field, one anti-tank, and one anti-aircraft regiments. The armoured car regiment was retained. The ratio of armour to infantry was now three to four.

The wheeled armoured car regiment was considered unsuitable for reconnaissance in European country, and for the invasion of Normandy it was replaced by an armoured reconnaissance regiment equipped with tanks. In addition, one of the two field artillery regiments and half the anti-tank regiment were equipped with self-propelled guns.

After the end of World War II the advent of the nuclear age led to much confused thinking. At first the organisation existing at the end of the war was retained, but the armoured brigade was increased in strength to four armoured regiments, whilst divisional reconnaissance was once again entrusted to an armoured car regiment. Before long there were further modifications. The infantry brigade was raised to four battalions, but later again reduced to three. Both artillery regiments and the anti-tank regiment (now Royal Armoured Corps) were equipped with self-propelled guns, but the latter unit was later abolished.

In 1955 the British Armoured divisions were once more reorganised, and this time in a most extraordinary fashion; the infantry component being so reduced as to result in a formation which war experience should have shown to be extremely ill-balanced. There were no brigade headquarters; instead, the four armoured regiments were directly under divisional headquarters. There was only one infantry battalion, one medium artillery regiment, and a regiment of armoured cars for reconnaissance. The armour to infantry ratio was therefore now four to one, or nearly back to 1939!

The next year one of these armoured divisions was broken up and its four armoured regiments were incorporated in the infantry divisions. At about the same time it was officially proclaimed that the role of the armoured division was limited to exploitation. No doubt there are many soldiers today who, looking at the mass of potentially hostile armour, only wish that that silly statement were true!

In 1957 the weakness of the new armoured division had presumably been appreciated, for in that year there was another even more radical reorganisation. The brigade was restored to favour but the division was abolished from the British Army. Instead there were two kinds of brigade group — armoured and infantry. The armoured brigade group was composed of three armoured regiments, one infantry battalion in armoured personnel carriers, one artillery regiment with 155mm SP howitzers, together with Royal Engineers, Royal Signals, and service units. The infantry brigade group was generally similar, but with three battalions of infantry and one armoured regiment. These two formations were copied from the Russian tank and mechanised infantry divisions respectively, and together gave an equal ratio of armour and infantry. It is difficult to see anything in favour of this organisation, which was quite foreign to all our war experience, and was obviously only suited to a power with such vast superiority in armour that it could be used as a battering ram with armour-assisted infantry follow up. In the British version of this organisation, divisional headquarters were retained to exercise command of any number of brigade groups of the two kinds.

By 1970 divisions were partially restored to favour and the Defence White Paper of that year cited the First British Corps in Germany as consisting of three divisions, each of two brigade groups, and corps troops of two artillery brigades and an armoured reconnaissance force. Four of the brigades had been reorganised to give a better balance of armour and mechanised infantry, and the reorganisation of a fifth was to be carried during the year.

In 1971 'brigade groups' had gone, and divisions were properly back. First British Corps now had (according to the Defence White Paper) three divisional headquarters, five armoured brigades, one mechanised brigade, and the same corps troops as in the previous year.

And so to the Defence Review of 1974, when it was decided that divisions should be made smaller, the brigade level of command eliminated, and combat units made larger. In some respects the new armoured division is a reversion to that of 1955 in the absence of brigade headquarters and a total of five armoured and mechanised infantry units. But the ratio is entirely different because there are only two armoured regiments as compared with three mechanised infantry battalions, and, as there is also a wheeled infantry battalion, the ratio of armour to infantry is two to four. However, with an armoured reconnaissance regiment in light tanks and a considerable amount of artillery, the division is not too dissimilar in its composition to that of the final years of the Second World War. But the system of command and tactical grouping is entirely different to anything tried previously.

The Second Armoured Division, the first of this new pattern, was formed in September 1976 under the command of Major-General F. Kitson, and he has given an admirable description of it in the Journal of the Royal United Services Institute.[1]

Nineteen years after its abolition the armoured division is back in the British Army, and in a main battle role 20 years after its official relegation to exploitation. When reinforced with units and men after mobilisation the division would have just under 14,000 men, as compared with Russian establishments of just under 13,000 men for a mechanised rifle division and just over 10,000 for a tank division.

The two armoured regiments are each composed of a headquarters squadron and four sabre squadrons, each of four troops with four Chieftain tanks apiece. In each of the three mechanised infantry battalions there is a headquarters company and four mechanised companies, each of three platoons, each of which has three sections, and all are carried in APCs. In the headquarters company is a mortar platoon of four sections armed with two 81mm mortars each, and an anti-tank platoon also of four sections each of which has four Milan ATGWs.

There are thus eight armoured squadrons and 12 mechanised companies, and from these 20 squadrons/companies are formed five battle groups; the ratio of armour to infantry in each will depend on the tactical situation. Each of these battle groups would have in addition a close reconnaissance troop from the armoured reconnaissance regiment, an anti-aircraft troop, and a long range anti-tank guided weapons troop. Each battle group is commanded by the headquarters of one of the armoured regiments or mechanised infantry battalions, and it is in effect a reduction of the brigade group to the lower level of a regimental or battalion group.

The armoured reconnaissance regiment has a headquarters squadron, two medium reconnaissance squadrons, and a close reconnaissance squadron. The medium reconnaissance squadrons undertake the functions of the divisional cavalry regiments, armoured car regiments, and reconnaissance regiments of the past. A squadron has four reconnaissance troops, each with four Scorpion light tanks, and a survey troop equipped with five Spartans which can be used either to carry assault sections or for survey, for which they are fitted with ZB 298 radars. In the close reconnaissance squadron are the five reconnaissance troops, of which one is allocated to each battle group. A close reconnaissance troop is equipped with eight Scimitar light tanks.

The wheeled infantry battalion has an organisation similar to that of the mechanised battalions, but its four rifle companies are not mechanised and all the vehicles are wheeled. In addition to this battalion a division may have some independent rifle companies.

The divisional artillery consists of three regiments, containing between them four batteries of Abbots, three batteries of 155mm SP medium guns, three batteries of towed 5.5in medium guns, and one battery of 8in M110 SP howitzers; each battery having six equipments. In addition the division would normally be allocated batteries of 175mm M107 SP heavy guns from the new Artillery Division. (This division made its first ever appearance in the British Army when it was formed in the First British Corps. Its function in battle is to provide long range heavy fire power for the Corps, and also to locate and engage enemy artillery and other targets, and to provide air defence cover. It has regiments equipped with 177mm heavy guns, Lance nuclear missiles, Drone pilotless aircraft, and Rapier anti-aircraft guided missiles.)[2] For air defence the armoured division gets a battery of Rapiers and two batteries of L40/70 Bofors, as well as Blowpipe air defence sections attached to each battle group.

The divisional engineers consist of two regiments, containing between them five field squadrons, a field support squadron, and a troop of armoured engineers. The value of engineer units is probably greater than ever, with the importance of mine laying, mine clearing, bridging, demolitions, etc. The more extensive the area to be defended the greater become the engineer tasks in the plan of defence.

The remaining elements of the armoured division are the divisional signal regiment, the Army Air Corps regiment, a transport regiment, an armoured workshop, an ordnance company, a provost company, and the divisional medical units consisting of two field ambulances and an ambulance squadron RCT.

The flexibility of this new style division is increased by the system of task forces. Instead of detailing brigades of fixed organisation to carry out the various parts of his plan, the divisional commander is now supposed to decide the tasks that need doing and to allocate a number of battle groups to each task. But because he cannot give orders to each battle group himself, while at the same time keeping control of events throughout his area, he has two deputies, each to take command of battle groups charged with a particular task, and the signal facilities to set up two task force headquarters. General Kitson points out, however, that although the new system is more flexible and more economical than the previous one, it is at the expense of the cohesion and mutual confidence which exists in fixed brigades where units train and fight together under the same commander.

As regards the occupation of a defensive position General Kitson believes that the depth of country for which a division is likely to be responsible may prove to be more of a difficulty than the width of its front. This is because the enemy may attack in depth by lifting troops in helicopters, supported by armed helicopters and fixed wing aircraft; a form of attack that would stretch the division's resources in keeping the main supply routes open and logistic units functioning in the rear areas.

As the composition of both battle groups and task forces can be changed to meet the situation, there are very many combinations that can be made to suit the terrain and the tactical problem. The wheeled infantry battalion and the medium reconnaissance regiment can be formidable in defence under the right conditions. So the divisional commander has a considerable number of options open to him in his probable three main tasks in a defensive position of covering his front, securing his rear areas, and providing a divisional reserve.

Another aspect of the new division is the change in the logistic organisation. Largely because of the abolition of brigades, the logistic resources are pooled and allocated by the divisional commander as required; and those for the support of the battle groups are not controlled by the task force commanders who exercise only operational command. Logistics, though, probably loom larger in importance today than ever before, owing to the enormous expenditure of ammunition and material on the modern battlefield. However, before dealing with the vital matters of supply and recovery, the tactical organisation of the armoured division will be examined a little more closely.

It would be strange if such a new and relatively untried system were not amended in some particulars in the light of experience — an expectation which is supported by the past history of armoured divisions.

The task force idea is excellent in principle, and it has been used very effectively by, for example, Marshal Davout at the battle of Auerstaedt in 1806[3] and Field Marshal Rommel in the Western Desert. But both Davout and Rommel formed their task forces from normal formations to meet particular contingencies as they arose, and once a contingency was over the normal formation was restored. One disadvantage of the task force as planned for the new armoured divisions has already been mentioned; another is that task forces will be formed before the tasks have been indentified, simply because there is not the time to wait. In other words, the old idea of forming a special task force to meet a situation which suddenly arises, is replaced by forming task forces anyway because the divisional commander cannot command without them.

In mobile warfare under present conditions there are obvious advantages in the close co-ordination of armour and mechanised infantry, and the battle group is a very good way of achieving it. But the present organisation of battle groups entails squadrons and regiments often fighting under other commands than that of their own regiment or battalion, and it is inherently unsound that troops should train under one command and fight under another. There is also the matter of regimental tradition and morale, for the squadron or company becomes the fighting unit rather than the regiment.

A third difficulty arises over the organisation of close reconnaissance; for the armoured regiment loses the responsibility for training its own reconnaissance troop. The importance which an armoured regiment attaches to a reconnaissance troop has been vividly portrayed by Brigadier H. B.C. Watkins. He writes:

'I remember very well how in the 1st Royal Tank Regiment in 1944-45, our CO placed so much reliance upon the reconnaissance troop that of the eight patrols..., four were commanded by officers and the remainder by sergeants. Thanks to the efforts of these picked men we were seldom unaware of the position on our front or to our flanks, every major movement of the regiment was carefully recced and every regimental axis clearly marked... From World War II onwards the tradition of the elite character of the recce troops was perpetuated... There has always been a need for route recce and marking if time was not to be lost during tactical movement, particularly at night. Within the armoured regiment this is a prime task for the recce troop and calls for the highest standards of training and initiative... The training of a first class recce troop is not done overnight. Because... it may often be necessary for a CO to rely absolutely upon the accuracy of the report and soundness of the judgement of a junior NCO, or even of an experienced trooper, the officers, NCOs and soldiers of these recce troops must be handpicked. Of course it is possible to command an armoured regiment in battle using recce support from an outside source, but the task of the CO is thereby made immeasurably more difficult...'[4]

This is a strong case against incorporating the close reconnaissance troops in the armoured reconnaissance regiment, because it would be trying human nature too far to expect the commanding officer of an armoured reconnaissance regiment to put his best men into troops which are destined to leave his command as soon as operations start.

Because this book looks towards the Army of tomorrow as well as today, one could perhaps hazard guesses as to how the organisation of the Armoured division might change as a result of exercises and studies. A solution to the battle group problem might lie in having smaller units but more of them. A smaller type armoured regiment, for instance, might have three sabre squadrons each of three troops, instead of four sabre squadrons each of four troops, and a smaller mechanised battalion might have three mechanised companies instead of four. With the existing 20 squadrons/companies the average battle group has four of them. With the suggested smaller units one armoured regiment and one mechanised battalion could be permanently associated to form a battle group when required, commanded by the senior of the two lieutenant-colonels. The size of such a battle group would not differ significantly from an existing one because it would have 18 troops/platoons instead of 14.

Such standard battle groups might enable a return to the brigade. There could be three in a division, each of two armoured regiments and two mechanised battalions, that is two battle groups; so that a division would have six battle groups instead of the present five. To meet the reconnaissance difficulty each armoured regiment and each mechanised battalion might have its own reconnaissance troop/platoon.

Some such organisation could result in:

a   Greater mutual confidence in battle through having a fixed command system, and through units of a fixed battle group training together.
b   More effective cover of wide frontages, because this is easier with, say, two small units rather than with one big one.
c   Higher morale in regiments and battalions, who would prefer to fight as such rather than be split up.
d   More reliable communications because the divisional signal regiment would be serving fixed headquarters with reasonably standard groupings.

These forecasts of the shape of the armoured division of tomorrow may well be wide of the mark, but the importance of arriving at a satisfactory organisation and balance of all arms can hardly be over-emphasised.

136

Logistics

The bulk of ammunition and equipment for BAOR comes by sea and is delivered overland by train and truck. Fuel and oil, however, are supplied by the Central Europe Pipeline System (CEPS), which came into operation in 1958, and, after initial use for aviation fuel, now transports and stores both ground and aviation fuel for NATO forces. The system is managed by the Central Europe Operating Agency (CEOA) at Versailles; one of the few NATO organisations still in France. The CEOA manages it through seven pipeline divisions, each of which is staffed by the country through which the pipeline runs; Belgium, France, Germany, or the Netherlands. It has signal communications with the military headquarters and organisations which are concerned with the supply of petrol, oil, and lubricants (POL). The system has about 6,000km of pipeline buried about a metre deep, and duplicated at river crossings and other places where repair would be difficult. Fuel is fed into the system at entry points from a refinery. British fuel normally goes in at Antwerp, Marseilles and Rotterdam. It is then pumped by some of the 105 pumping stations to one or more of the 53 bulk storage depots, and thence as needed to national depots and airbases. Three different types of fuel are delivered by the system. There is no gap between them in the pipe, a 'slug' of one kind being followed often by one of another kind. But although some mixing inevitably occurs it can be identified and the mixture is transferred at a depot to contamination tanks and returned for purification and re-issue. Installations are protected by reinforced concrete, and the facilities for rerouting and for drawing from a number of different depots provide insurance against a considerable amount of damage.[5]

At 'pipehead' the Royal Corps of Transport has a Composite Maintenance Group, and from here fuel is carried forward in bulk by 4 ton Fuel (Dispensing) Tanker Trucks, designed for dispensing ground fuels direct into vehicle service tanks. The single compartment steel carrier tank has a capacity for 800gal. These trucks, and those carrying ammunition, supplies, etc, go to the Replenishment Parks in the Corps area, and then forward to Exchange Points in the divisional areas. The next move forward is to the Intermediate Replenishment Groups, which are in immediate support of the divisional artillery and the battle groups, thus replacing the old Brigade Administrative Areas. The whole of this movement is carried out by RCT vehicles, and the last stage is the responsibility of the divisional transport regiment.[6] The most recent experience of war between opponents armed with modern weapons was the Yom Kippur war of October 1973, when 'the rates of attrition on the battlefield and the general consumption of ammunition of all natures went far beyond anything to be found in previous military experience.'[7] This is the measure of the problems with which the RCT, REME, RAOC, and, indeed, RAMC will be faced.

REME is in a way the reverse of the RCT in that its main problem is evacuation rather than delivery. The REME recovery system in the field is organised in four stages which are linked to a line of workshops. These stages, from front to rear, are equipment collecting points (ECPs), backloading points (BLPs), recovery posts, and workshops.

In an armoured regiment there is an armoured recovery vehicle (ARV) in each sabre squadron and one in regimental reserve. These ARVs belong to the REME light aid detachment (LAD) attached to the armoured regiment and they carry out first line recovery; that is to say, maintenance of tank mobility, assistance at obstacle crossings (such as minefields), and towing casualties to an ECP or a safe area. The next stage is second line recovery which is controlled by the divisional Commander Royal Electrical and Mechanical Engineers (CREME), who allots resources as they are needed. Second line responsibilities include clearing the routes forward of the divisional rear area, assisting at defiles, bridges, etc, reinforcing the first line when needed, moving heavy armoured vehicles to second line workshops or divisional BLPs, and clearing the battlefield. Third line recovery includes moving vehicles from second line workshops or divisional BLPs to the heavier third line workshops or to Corps BLPs. Fourth line recovery is the final stage — backloading vehicles from Corps to Base.[8]

The Royal Air Force

It may perhaps appear surprising to include a section on the Royal Air Force in a book about the Army, particularly in a chapter dealing with the armoured division; but the RAF is so closely concerned with the land battle that the part it plays must be included. The NATO tactical air forces operate in very close conjunction with the land forces and are commanded from Joint Command Operations Centres which are established at the Army Group/Tactical Air Force level (eg NORTHAG/2ATAF). From such a centre aircraft are allocated for counter-air action, interdiction (ie attack on enemy supports and reserve), and reconnaissance for a set period — say the next six or 12 hours. Some air effort may be delegated for a similar period to a corps headquarters, where there are Air Support Operations Centres (ASOC). This has the advantage that by establishing communications between corps headquarters and squadrons of fighter/ground attack aircraft, the briefing given to pilots on the tactical situation is likely to be up to date, and, furthermore, the response will be quicker.

Typical requirements for air support are:

a   Tactical reconnaissance. This will be a prime requirement by a commander holding a wide front against an enemy in superior strength, in order that he may identify enemy threats and redeploy forces, if necessary, to counter them.

b   Interdiction. A typical task would be to attack enemy armoured columns before they have deployed in the battle area.

c   Close air support. That is, direct participation in the land battle; perhaps to stem an enemy armoured breakthrough, or to assist our forces to disengage from one defensive positions and withdraw to another. The last of these is the most difficult because of the pilots' difficulties in distinguishing friend from foe on the ground. To assist in this there is a Forward Air Controller (FAC), and his first problem is to get to the right place at the right time to direct the close air support. His second problem is to work with the attack pilot to bring about a successful attack.[9] (The use of laser designators by FACs is dealt with in Chapter 11.)

The White Paper lists 12 RAF squadrons in Germany. Of these, six consist of Buccaneers and Jaguars for strike/attack, one has Jaguars for reconnaissance, two have Harriers for offensive support, two have Phantoms for air defence, and one has Wessex helicopters for air transport.

The aircraft, therefore, with which the Army is likely to be most closely associated is the Harrier. Its most valuable characteristic is its short take-off and landing run, though it has acquired fame from its ability to rise vertically. Although the latter may occasionally confer great operational advantage, there is a severe penalty in the reduction of the load that can be carried. It is likely to be the exception, therefore, rather than the rule.

Most NATO aircraft require concrete runways 6,000ft in length (though the Jaguar can take off in less than 3,000ft of grass.) Harrier, with its maximum weapon load, only needs a grass ground roll of 800ft and then has a radius of action of about 150 nautical miles. In the vertical mode a Harrier can carry only some 40% of its maximum weapon load and its radius of action is reduced to about 50 nautical miles.

Because of their ability to take off vertically, Harriers could be widely dispersed locally when any diplomatic tension arose, and would be far less vulnerable to surprise attack than other aircraft; and they could operate from several dispersed sites.

For use against armour Harriers would probably carry the cluster bomb. Five cluster bombs could be carried in addition to the aircraft's guns. Harriers would probably operate in pairs, covering quite a large area, and the discovery of an enemy tank column moving in close order along a road would present them with an ideal target. The ratio of cluster bombs dropped to the number of tanks knocked out would depend on the dispersal between the tanks, but any single target would have no chance of survival. As a target for enemy aircraft, a Harrier with its ability to hover, move sideways — even backwards, attacking at low level and accelerating way at about 600kts would be a very difficult object to hit.[10]

15

The Enemy

This chapter of this book on the British Army is devoted to the enemy which it is being trained and equipped to fight, should that enemy ever be tempted to convert the hostile manoeuvres of these recent, and not so recent, years into open hostilities against the North Atlantic Alliance.

Anybody who has the temerity to suggest the pattern of a future war is on exceptionally difficult ground, because prophets, both official and amateur, have usually been hopelessly wrong in their forecasts, and never more so than before the start of each of the two world wars. Nevertheless, some deductions can be made from the effects of modern weapons in the Arab-Israeli fighting and from the equipment, strength, and tactical doctrine of our only conceivable opponents.

If the British Army has to fight, the major part of it will presumably do so on the North German plain. It is a terrain which, in spite of its name, is not unsuitable for defence, for the one-time open tank country is now dotted with villages and small townships which are only separated from each other by some three kilometres and are therefore, if occupied by troops, within mutually supporting distance.[1] As against this, the very wide fronts which the forces of the NATO Central Europe Command have to hold favour the armies of the Warsaw Pact because, as they would be the aggressors, they would be able to choose their points of attack and concentrate at them rapidly and with little warning. Further, as stated in Chapter 13, this advantage might enable them to achieve the enormous local superiority of 20 or 30 to one in each of four or five separate thrusts.[2]

The top priority of the defending forces at this stage, therefore, would be to obtain rapid information of enemy concentrations and movements in order to effect their own concentrations or re-deployments in time to counter the anticipated thrusts.[3]

The Warsaw Pact forces also have the advantage of being able to choose the weapons. It is a fallacy to suppose that the strategy of 'flexible response' means that NATO can decide when and if tactical nuclear weapons should be used. The Russians have no conception of a deterrent or of a graduated response. If it appears to them that it would be worth their while to use tactical weapons from the start of hostilities, they would probably do so. On the other hand, since NATO can respond in kind, they might well decide to rely on their considerable superiority in conventional weapons to gain their objectives. The use of chemical weapons is another matter. Against those NATO formations which were not equipped with these weapons the Soviet command might order their use from the start in order to compel NATO troops to wear protective clothing, whilst their own soldiers fought free of such encumbrance.[4]

Current Russian tactical doctrine is that the opposing defence can be penetrated by surprise and swift manoeuvre, though if this failed it would be replaced by massive armoured frontal attack by tanks and mechanised infantry. The latter are carried in the so-called BMPs and the later MTLBs, which are more than just armoured personnel carriers, because they carry a considerable armament and the Soviet infantry are normally expected to fight in them and not to dismount. The BMP mounts a 73mm anti-tank gun and an ATGW, whilst the MTLB has a larger gun of 76mm. In the opening moves of a Soviet attempt at a swift penetration by surprise and manoeuvre, the task of the BMPs would be to open the way for the tanks by knocking out the opposing anti-tank guns and guided weapons. The units for such tactics are combined arms groups based on mechanised infantry regiments and composed of quite small combat teams of BMPs, tanks, and SP guns.[5] Behind these light forces would come the main bodies, the attack on each axis being led by the tank regiments of a tank division, operating on a divisional front between two and eight kilometres wide. Close behind the leading tank battalions would come mechanised rifle companies of the tank division in BMPs to tackle the opposing tank defences. Following the tank division would be a motor rifle division to exploit the breakthrough and swing against the opponent's flanks in order to clear a path for the tank and motor rifle divisions of the next echelon, which would be pushing ahead to maintain the impetus of the advance.[6]

That is the theory, and it appears simple in execution, but as Clausewitz says, in a well-known passage:

'Everything is very simple in war, but the simplest thing is difficult. These difficulties accumulate and produce a friction which no man can imagine who has not seen war ... Friction is the only conception which in a general way corresponds to that which distinguishes real war from war on paper ... This enormous friction, which is not concentrated, as in mechanics, at a few points, is therefore everywhere brought into contact with chance, and thus incidents take place upon which it was impossible to calculate, their chief origin being chance.'[7]

Provided, however, that Soviet commanders are adequate, that junior leaders can exercise initiative, that the training of tank crews and infantry is thorough, that communications work, and that logistics are properly organised, there should be some penetration at least, and it seems that very mobile battles, fought over an area of considerable depth, would result. Judging by the Yom Kippur War of 1973, the rates of attrition on such a battlefield are likely to be appalling. In that conflict the general consumption of ammunition of all natures went far beyond anything to be found in previous military experience. The Syrian and Egyptian armies together outnumbered the Israelis by 3 to 1 in tanks, 2 to 1 in aircraft, 25 to 1 in surface to air missiles (SAMs), and at least 2 to 1 in manpower.[8] This is not unlike the superiority which the Warsaw Pact have over the NATO forces in Central Europe, and it indicates the importance of generalship, training, and morale as the only adequate counter.

The tank battles on both the Golan Heights and in Sinai were on a greater scale than any in World War II. For instance, at Alamein the Germans had 600 tanks against 1,350 British, and during the battle the Germans lost 450 tanks and the British 350, as well as 150 disabled. In the 1973 war the Israelis had about 1,700 tanks, the Egyptians 2,500 and the Syrians 1,300. Losses were Israeli 820 and the Arabs together 1,350. The Israeli M48, M60 and Centurion tanks proved superior to the Russian T-54/55s and T-62s, but the Egyptian anti-tank missiles particularly the Russian Saggers, took a heavy toll of the Israeli tanks. On the Golan Heights, of the tank losses, 80% were from tank guns 10% from ATGWs, and 10% from artillery, mines, etc.[10] This is o: some interest, but if the Israelis had had the Milan ATGW and the Ba: Mine the two latter percentages might have been a lot higher.

The Soviet command is of course fully aware of the above figures an of the logistic resources needed to keep an armoured thrust going Armoured replenishment columns which are self-contained, fast-moving and capable of looking after themselves are a likely development.[11] Needless to say, these columns would be very important interdiction targets for the tactical air forces.

It is worth while taking a closer look at the Yom Kippur War, because both Syrians and Egyptians were armed with Soviet equipment and were trained in Soviet tactical methods. The Syrian objective was the recapture of the Golan Heights. They intended to mount a surprise attack and so complete the operation within 24 hours; which, they estimated, would be before the Israelis had time to mobilise and reinforce. They attacked at 1400 hours on 6 October 1973, achieving indeed their surprise, but things then went wrong. At that time the Israelis had 177 tanks on the Heights, against which the Syrians could bring over 1,100. The Israeli position, some 30 miles in length, consisted of a string of fortified volcanic mounds along the ridge, separated from each other by a mile or two and each manned by a weak platoon of infantry and an artillery OP. They were in fact merely a covering force.

The initial Syrian attack was carried out by three mechanised brigades, each of which included a tank battalion with 40 tanks. The infantry battalions of these brigades were carried in Russian APCs, in which, it was intended, they would fight instead of dismounting. This was therefore the standard Russian tactical doctrine; the surprise attack and the mechanised brigades sweeping away the covering troops with their anti-tank weapons to clear the way for the armoured thrust. It did not work like that. The mechanised brigades surrounded and by-passed the Israeli strong points but did not succeed in taking any of them, while the OPs called down the supporting Israeli artillery fire. That night four Syrian armoured brigades with 120 tanks each were thrown into the battle, and by midday on 7 October a Syrian armoured division with another three brigades joined in the attack. By that time, however, the Israeli armoured reinforcements were arriving and the Israeli Air Force was pounding Syrian columns. At the end of the battle the Syrians withdrew, having lost over 1,000 tanks destroyed or captured.[12]

In Sinai the Egyptians also attacked at 1400 hours on 6 October. They had the more difficult problem of crossing the Suez Canal, a formidable water obstacle. Beyond this was also a line of strong points — the so-called Bar Lev line, some 75 miles long and manned by a covering force of only about 500 men.

The Egyptians had rehearsed this crossing on models and exercises, and they put it into practice with remarkable success, achieving complete surprise and capturing a number of the Israeli strong points. The Israeli Air Force tried to destroy the crossings, but failed, and lost a large number of aircraft, brought down by guided missiles and the efficient ZSU-23-4 anti-aircraft guns mentioned in Chapter 10. As at the Golan Heights, the Yom Kippur commemoration hampered the Israeli mobilisation, and their main forces came into action without adequate preparation or organisation. Thus an armoured brigade attacked without infantry or proper artillery support and was almost entirely destroyed by a massive concentration of anti-tank guns, missiles, and grenades. Subsequent fighting on this front was defensive until the battle of the Golan Heights was over and the Israeli forces there could be switched south.[13]

Perhaps one of the most interesting aspects of the fighting up till this point lay in the use of the APCs. Both Egyptians and Syrians had been trained in the Russian system of fighting in the APCs and 'closed down'. The Israelis also preferred their infantry fighting mounted, but with their head and shoulders outside, where they could see better. Many Syrian APCs were destroyed with their infantry still inside them. A large number of Israeli APCs were also destroyed or immobilised, and their infantry, when forced to dismount, were not well trained to fight on foot. In defence the Israeli APCs were used more effectively in combination with the tanks. The latter lay back in concealed positions, firing at the enemy armour, whilst the APCs took on the hostile infantry and guided missile teams.[14]

Opinion is divided in the NATO armies on the use of APCs. Some prefer their infantry to fight mounted, but in the British Army it is the normal practice, of course, to fight dismounted, using the APCs to carry the infantry into action in the old mounted infantry tradition. Every infantry weapon is more effective when fired from the ground, and it is easier to knock out a thinly armoured APC than to kill all the men of a well trained infantry section in firing positions on the ground. The Yom Kippur War was fought in mainly very open country, but where the country is close, the ground rough, and the visibility limited by buildings, vegetation, weather or darkness, the infantryman on foot is far more efficient than one mounted in a vehicle.[15]

The Israeli counter-attack and crossing of the Suez Canal is a fine illustration of the part that generalship can play in a battle against greatly superior numbers. Sites had been selected for the crossing before war broke out, and one of these was chosen for the attempt. The plan was for General Arik Sharon's division to get over the Canal and hold a bridgehead through which two other divisions could pass. Sharon's bridgehead was to be immediately north of the Bitter Lake, which would protect his left flank, and, as it happened, it was also the boundary between the 2nd and 3rd Egyptian Armies. For the crossing a bridge, 200m long, had been built before hand, and this was towed across the desert by tanks. Sharon started at dusk on 15 October and, with diversionary attacks and movements to mislead the Egyptians, he was over the Canal with 200 men by midnight. Hard fighting followed on the east bank to hold the access roads, and under this cover the bridge was launched and the Israeli plan succeeded.[16]

In the light of their experience, most Israeli generals believe that the art of generalship lies in timing.[17] One perhaps thinks immediately of Salamanca, and of Wellington's close scrutiny of the move of Marmont's army till, seeing a gap open in the enemy's line of march, he exclaimed: 'By God! That will do!' and hurled Packenham's division into the attack. Marshal Maurice de Saxe knew it. He writes of a general in battle:

'When at last he sees his fair lady of opportunity, he should kiss her hand and go at once to the critical spot, striking hard with the first troops on which he can lay hands. It is thus that decisive victory is gained. I do not suggest how or when this should be done because it will depend on a variety of situations and positions which can arise in battle and indicate the opportunity. The art is to see and know how to profit by it . . . '[18]

The training of a soldier in what to expect is an important part of the preparation for war. Clausewitz put it neatly when he wrote: 'It is of immense importance that the soldier, high or low, whatever rank he has, should not have to encounter in war those things which, when seen for the first time, set him in astonishment and perplexity.'[19] One hopes that in any future conflcit British soldiers will be neither astonished nor perplexed.

Having discussed Soviet material and tactics, one may perhaps consider the Soviet soldier. Most men in the ranks are conscripts, serving for a period of two years. On conscription they generally go to a holding unit for basic training before being posted to a field unit for collective and specialist training. As in all conscript armies, field units are essentially training establishments, and with a two-year term of service, nearly a quarter of the strength leave for the reserve every six months. Training has its difficulties, for there are over 100 different nationalities in the USSR, each with its own language and some with their own alphabet. To avoid encouraging any national spirit, these different peoples are dispersed throughout the Army, so that communication between instructor and recruit is not always easy. Three-quarters of Soviet soldiers are townsmen, because there is a shortage of young men on the land. Their civilian standard of living, therefore, is a good deal higher than they receive in the ranks of the Army. These town dwellers, too, do not have the stamina of the peasant soldiers of an earlier generation, and a lot of time has to be devoted to physical training. Discipline is very strict, and a conscript does not get any leave during his two years service.

NCOs are selected from the ranks and may be sent for six months to a NCO training unit. If a NCO signs on for a further period of service he is allowed special privileges. The Soviet Army is, however, weak in the standard of its NCOs — a weakness which is appreciated and which has led to the introduction of the rank of ensign. This is half way between NCO and officer and not really equivalent to warrant officer. NCOs can be promoted to ensign and the latter may become officers; and indeed do become reserve officers on completing their active service.

About 20% of the officers are promoted either from ensigns or from the two-year conscripts. Most of the remainder come from educational establishments or from industry, and a few are reservists granted a short service commission. A junior Russian officer is not expected to have much initiative, and tactical training and doctrine is limited to preparation for only one type of war. Much of the junior officer's time is spent in the political education of the men under his command.

Russian soldiers have always been hardy and stubborn fighters, but they have also always been lazy with little sense of urgency, and they are easily depressed if things go wrong.[20]

In World War II, according to some German soldiers who fought against them, the average Russian soldier was quite lacking in initiative and no good at all unless properly led.[21] One gains the impression that the above are characteristics of Russian soldiers throughout the ages, for they could be applied equally to the solid battalion masses that were beaten by the British infantry at the Alma and at Inkermann in 1854.

16

The Army in Northern Ireland

The last two chapters have been concerned with the primary role of the British Army, that is the defence of the interests of ourselves and our allies against an attack by the Soviet Union and its satellites in the Warsaw Pact. Nevertheless, although the Army has been engaged in a number of operations of various kinds since the end of World War II, none of them was more than limited in their scope. They have included such actions as the United Nations' war in Korea, the Mau-Mau rebellion, the anti-communist campaign in Malaya, the insurgency in Aden, the Suez campaign, the confrontation with Indonesia, the expedition to Anguilla, peace-keeping in Cyprus, the counter to threats against Belize, and many others of a minor nature. Longer-lasting than all of these has been the insurgency in Northern Ireland.

It is apparent from the above brief record of events that the British Army has a secondary role of dealing with contingencies short of major war, and that these contingencies can be subdivided into limited war in any part of the world and counter-insurgency at home or overseas. If the Soviet Union should see the latter as the cheapest and most promising aid to its ambition of world domination, then it may be the type of conflict in which the British Army is most likely to be engaged in the years to come.

Northern Ireland — the Background

Insurgency in Ireland is no new thing, and the original causes are still hotly disputed. It is not intended to examine them here: indeed they are irrelevant, because the extremists on both sides — Protestants and Catholics; Orangemen and Nationalists — have been brought up on historical myths which have little in common with history.

The more immediate origin of the present emergency lies in the Easter rebellion of 1916. After the suppression of this, there followed a period of guerrilla warfare against British rule by the original Irish Republican Army. In 1920 the Government of Ireland Act established two separate states with Parliaments in Belfast and Dublin respectively, each subordinate to Westminster. The northern state consisted of six of Ulster's nine counties, whilst in the southern state were the remaining 26. This political organisation was accepted reluctantly in the North but rejected in the South, and the guerrilla war continued. Following a truce in the fighting, the South was offered Dominion Status, and this amendment to the original proposal was accepted by a narrow majority and incorporated in an Anglo-Irish Treaty. Civil war then broke out between the new Irish Free State Government and the Republican Party who refused to accept the treaty. The Government won and in 1925 recognised the border with Northern Ireland as delineated in the 1920 Act. The Irish Free State remained neutral in World War II, and in 1948 it severed the British connection by declaring a Republic.

The Anglo-Irish Treaty and the termination of the Civil War did not end the hostility of a section of the community to the separation of North and South, and a new Irish Republican Army came into being, dedicated to removing the border by force of arms. This force, which had little or no connection with the old IRA, established units of varying and fluctuating strengths in Belfast and other parts of Northern Ireland.

IRA gangs staged a number of incidents in country areas in the 1930s, and the administrative movement of small parties of troops on certain roads was prohibited in case of attempts to seize their arms.

Every year on 12 July the Protestant Orange Order commemorates the victory gained by William of Orange at the Battle of the Boyne. There are processions with bands throughout Northern Ireland. On that date in 1935 an Orange procession marched through a Nationalist quarter of Belfast, and in the resultant clashes IRA gunmen killed some 12 Orangemen. The burial of the first of these victims was attended by an angry mob, who announced their intention of smashing up the Falls Road after the funeral. An appeal by the Royal Ulster Constabulary for assistance was answered by the despatch of a platoon of the 60th Rifles to the Falls Road, accompanied by the Author with a wireless truck. The RUC, at whom some of the mob had been firing, fell back through the 60th; but the sight of the soldiers standing at ease with fixed bayonets was too much for the mass of marchers, who turned away down a side street which had been left clear for that purpose. The normally hostile inhabitants of the Falls Road came out of their houses with cups of tea and cakes for the troops.

This was the start of riots all over Belfast, but the Government's action was rapid and firm. The Army moved in to help the RUC and took over sections in the centre of the City from the police. Barricades were erected in roads where the two communities met to keep them apart and a curfew was imposed and rigidly enforced. In three weeks it was all over, and the subsequent peace was once more disturbed only by minor incidents.

There was more disturbance after World War II. In 1951, for instance, the IRA broke into the armoury of the Territorial Battalion of The Royal Inniskilling Fusiliers at Ebrington Barracks in Londonderry, and it was the Author's unpleasant task to preside over the subsequent court of enquiry.

IRA violence was fairly continuous between 1956 and 1962, but this campaign subsided eventually owing to lack of support. The present campaign may be said to have started on 5 October 1968 when supporters of the Northern Ireland Civil Rights Association staged a march in Londonderry during which there was rioting. The NICA was soon dominated by the IRA which was now under communist control and the increasing number of riots that occurred gradually became beyond the power of the RUC to control. The Ulster Special Constabulary, or 'B Specials', were called out and eventually the help of the Army was requested.

The Security Forces in Northern Ireland at this time consisted of the Royal Ulster Constabulary and the 39th Brigade which included one armoured car regiment and two infantry battalions. The RUC were armed and trained as a semi-military force, or gendarmerie, and were about 3,400 strong. The B Specials were a part-time force with strength of about 8,500. There had been originally three types of Ulster Special Constabulary; the A Specials who provided full-time support for the RUC, the B Specials who were part-time, and the C Specials who were older men and unarmed. The A and C Specials had long since been disbanded. The RUC was a non-sectarian force, with several senior officers amongst the Catholics in it, but the B Specials were all Presbyterians and their impartiality was suspect by the Roman Catholic community.[1]

On 24 August 1969 a Royal Commission was set up under Lord Hunt to consider the future structure of the RUC. It recommended that the RUC itself should be disarmed and restricted to law enforcement and that the B Specials should be disbanded. In place of the latter it proposed that a new part-time military force under the Ministry of Defence should be raised; and this, the Ulster Defence Regiment would be non-sectarian, recruiting both Protestants and Catholics. At the same time as the Hunt commission was examining the structure of the RUC, another commission under Mr Justice Scarman was looking into its conduct. This radical alteration in the status of such a proud and well-trained force as the RUC, together with the reduction of its recently increased establishment of 5,000 to 3,000, and with the Scarman report still awaited, had a demoralising effect. In fact the Scarman commission found that the RUC had carried out their duties well under extremely difficult circumstances, and in due course the RUC was rearmed in October 1971 after six of the force had been murdered.[2]

In October 1970 there was an interesting split in the IRA. The leadership of this body and of the Sinn Fein political wing had become increasingly Marxist, and now advocated the overthrow of the Government in Dublin as well as that in Belfast. Those members of the IRA (the majority) who adhered to the traditional and more limited objective of abolishing the border, broke away from the parent body, the 'Official' IRA, to form a separate 'Provisional' IRA. Conflicts between the two soon followed, but the Provisionals rapidly became far the stronger.

The Army

The Army in Northern Ireland was called upon to act in aid of the Civil Power, and this is still its legal status. As the 'Statement on Defence Estimates 1978' puts it, the Army's operations are carried out in furtherance of the Government's policy for security in Northern Ireland which 'continues to be based on the development of the Royal Ulster Constabulary (RUC) as the instrument for the maintenance of law and order. The Armed Forces, including the Ulster Defence Regiment (UDR), will remain as the essential buttress of this policy for as long as is necessary.'

The Army has an extremely difficult role in Northern Irland. To quell an insurgency it is necessary to get the majority of the population on the side of the Government, that is to dispel any sympathy with the aims of the insurgents. It follows that over zealous action by the Security Forces could defeat its own object by incurring hostility. Restrained action, however, needs more troops. As Major-General F. E. Kitson has so well stated it, 'The number of troops required to control a given situation goes up as the amount of force which it is politically acceptable for them to use goes down.'[3]

Special training of the soldier is necessary because his task is so different to that for which his normal training prepares him. In action against enemy soldiers in regular warfare his duties are clear, and they include killing or otherwise putting out of action as many of his opponents as possible. On internal security duties within the United Kingdom he is subject, like any other citizen, to the Civil Law, and he must not kill or injure anyone unless the circumstances clearly require it. Such conditions are testing for morale and they demand a high standard of discipline and the confidence that comes from good leadership and professional knowledge and ability. Pride in the regiment and its traditions and the feeling of belonging to a rather select military family have a large part to play when the soldier is called upon to live under trying conditions, taunted and provoked by hostile civilians, and subject to attack by missiles thrown by seen assailants and shots fired by unseen ones. Self-control is an expendable asset and periods of duty in the Province are limited to four months.

The training of a unit for its primary role suffers of course from these periods in Northern Ireland. Although the posting is only for four months, two months preliminary training in internal security is needed, and with movement, leave, and other factors the time lost to collective training may be up to seven months. The Defence White Paper, quoted above, says that in Northern Ireland 'A total of 47 major units served during 1977. Nine major units have completed six tours of duty there and six units have completed seven tours.' These figures demonstrate the sacrifice in normal training. There are, of course, considerable benefits. The individual soldier acquires the alertness and efficiency which used to come from service on the North-West Frontier of India,

and junior leaders gain immeasurably in initiative and ability to command. The result is that the British Regular Army is now the finest counter-insurgency force in the world, and in present world conditions the value of this can hardly be overestimated.

The strength of the Army in Northern Ireland has been increased considerably since the early days of the insurgency, and it has fluctuated according to requirements. The White Paper states that in 1978 there were 13 major units of infantry, armour, and artillery. In detail, there were three brigade headquarters (including their signal squadrons), one armoured reconnaissance regiment, three engineer squadrons, four resident infantry battalions, eight units in an infantry role, one Special Air Service squadron, two squadrons of the Army Air Corps, and 11 battalions of the Ulster Defence Regiment.

The Ulster Defence Regiment

The Ulster Defence Regiment was created on 1 April 1970, with instructions to form seven battalions, one from each of the six counties and one in Belfast. As regards the counties, they were in alphabetical order, as follows: 1st Co Antrim, 2nd Co Armagh, 3rd Co Down, 4th Co Fermanagh, 5th Co. Londonderry and 6th Co Tyrone. The City of Belfast Battalion was the 7th. Recruiting was so good that in 1971 the 8th Battalion was formed in East Tyrone by dividing the 6th Battalion, and early in 1972 the 9th Battalion in the south of Co Antrim and the 10th Battalion in west Belfast were formed from the 1st and 7th Battalions respectively. Finally, the 11th Craigavon Battalion was formed from parts of the 2nd and 3rd Battalions to take over operations in the industrial estate of Craigavon and the western parts of Co Down.[4]

The task of the Regiment was 'to support the Regular forces in Northern Ireland, should circumstances so require, in protecting the border and State against armed attack and sabotage.' In order to ensure its religious impartiality, an Advisory Council of six prominent public men, of whom three were Protestants and three Catholics, was set up under the chairmanship of the Colonel Commandant of the Regiment to advise the General Officer Commanding Northern Ireland.[5] The executive head of the Regiment is a Regular officer with the rank of brigadier, designated the Commander Ulster Defence Regiment. His headquarters are in the same locality as HQ Northern Ireland.

In the first week of formation there were 5,393 applications for membership, and in the first few months of its existence more than half of the soldiers in the Regiment were former B Specials. Of the other, some 1,100 had previous military service, whilst about 1,500 were young men with no previous military or police experience.[6] Great care is taken over the acceptance of recruits. A special board has been set up and each applicant to appear before it must have two sponsors as to his character and security clearance from the RUC.[7]

Battalions are generally commanded by Regular officers, and there is a battalion staff of Regulars consisting of a training major, a quartermaster, a regimental sergeant-major, and a permanent staff instructor (signals). There is also in each battalion an adjutant and an administrative officer, both of whom are full-time officers of the UDR; the battalion second in command and the company commanders are part-time UDR officers.[8] The headdress of the Regiment is a green beret with the badge of a silver harp surmounted by a crown.

Enlistment of women into the UDR began in August 1973. They are employed mainly in searching female civilians, radio operating, manning operations rooms, maintaining statistics at vehicle check points, and accompanying night patrols. The high pitched voices of the radio operators led to them being named 'Greenfinches', and this nickname was soon applied to all the women members of the UDR. They are, incidentally, the only women soldiers who do not belong to the WRAC. By the end of 1975 there were 600 of them and a number have been commissioned as officers. Full-time women officers are employed as assistant adjutants and assistant operations officers, whilst part-time officers command the detachments of the WUDR.[9]

Soldiers of the UDR live at home, and are therefore especially vulnerable to attacks by the IRA. By the end of 1976 67 of them had been murdered and there have been more murders since. The Regiment is difficult to get into, but it takes a special type of courage to remain in it.

Personal Protection

The standard combat dress is inadequate for internal security operations because the restriction on more than limited retaliatory action makes the soldier a more than usually vulnerable target. So-called 'flak' jackets or vests give city patrols protection against blast and fragments, and a heavier version has been introduced for soldiers in observation posts or other duty which does not need much movement, and this is very effective against low velocity bullets.[10] To provide secure observation posts the 'sangar', so familiar to soldiers who have served on the North-West Frontier of India, has been revived. But whereas sangars on the Frontier were built of boulders and stones, those in Northern Ireland are constructed of earth-filled sandbags and timber, with an overhead protection of .25in steel plate. For defence against sporadic small arms fire the walls need to be .5m thick, but against more intensive fire .75m is necessary. Now that the IRA armoury includes rockets with HEAT warheads, which have great penetrating power against solid defences but soon lose their impetus if they first strike a protective screen, pre-fabricated corrugated iron shields are erected some three to four metres beyond the sangar wall. These have the additional advantage of keeping at a distance small boys equipped by the IRA with nail bombs to throw at soldiers.[11]

Soldiers on riot duty require protection against stones, bottles, and other missiles hurled by the mobs. The face needs protection most, and it was decided to develop a transparent plastic visor. A substance called Makralon, which has been used by astronauts as a very effective shield against pieces of space rock, was chosen. Movable visors of this material were fitted to an IS version of the new combat helmet. Makralon proved so good that long shields of it were made to protect the whole body. It has been known to stop a revolver bullet.[12]

Weapons to use against mobs without causing more than minor injury presented another problem. CS gas and water cannon were used, but had their limitations. The best solution was found in the rubber bullet, or baton round, and its successor the plastic bullet. The rubber bullet is made of medium hard rubber 146mm long and can be used in any 38mm calibre riot gun or pistol. The Webley 38mm anti-riot gun can fire both types of bullet. It has a pistol grip but a rifle-type butt, which allows it to be fired from the shoulder. The barrel length of 246mm gives it a range of up to about 120m. Using an adjustable backsight, it is claimed that a normal firer can put all his shots within a 300mm circle at 40m.[13]

Armoured Fighting Vehicles

Saladins, Saracens, and Ferrets have played important roles in Northern Ireland. Saracen is the wheeled armoured personnel carrier which preceded the tracked FV 432, and was developed between 1950 and 1953. It has six wheels, all driven and a fine cross-country performance. Its silence and 45mph road speed have been of great value in internal security operations in Malaya, Borneo, Kenya, Cyprus, and Aden. Apart from its commander and driver, it can carry an infantry section of 10 men. A Browning machine gun is mounted in the one-man turret.[14] In Northern Ireland its armour protection had to be increased owing to the IRA's acquisition of American M1 Garand rifles with armour piercing ammunition.[15] The Saladin armoured car was developed in parallel with the Saracen APC and has essentially the same chassis with six-wheel drive. It was issued to reconnaissance regiments in 1955 and has been widely used in the same anti-insurgent operations as the Saracen. Periscopes are provided in the hull for closed down operation.[16]

The Ulster Defence Regiment has been issued with Shorland armoured cars on a scale of one or two with each company.[17] The Shorland was built as a private venture by Short Brothers and Harland in 1965-66. It has a long-wheelbase Landrover chassis covered with 8mm armour plating, and a manually operated turret, mounting a General Purpose machine gun. It was designed to provide a cheap and reliable armoured car for internal security action, particularly street fighting, where attack is normally limited to missiles such as bricks and petrol bombs and to small arms fire. It is the first such vehicle to be designed specifically for the urban guerrilla warfare which has become prevalent all over the world and it is remarkably successful. It has a six-cylinder Rover engine and a road speed of 60mph. Particular attention has been paid to crew comfort, with heating and cooling fans, and a crew compartment lined with foam padding and having a number of quick access safety hatches.[18]

The Border

The border between Northern Ireland and the Irish Republic presents a major problem. It is 261 miles long and is crossed by a number of major roads and lanes. It is unmarked and it is all too easy to cross it by accident. Many years ago a farmer of my acquaintance owned a field which had one gate in Northern Ireland and the other in the Irish Free State (as it was then). IRA gangs can cross the border from the Republic to raid and ambush, and flee back across it to safety where the troops cannot follow. From the start of the present campaign there was intensive patrolling along the border to try and curtail cross-border

movement. However, it was soon apparent that, with a border of such length and ease of passage, by the time troops could reach the locality of a reported incident or suspicious vehicle they might well be too late to intercept the terrorists. Helicopters were introduced to deal with the problem and proved invaluable. Army Air Corps Sioux reconnaissance helicopters operated along the border, keeping radio contact with their headquarters. Any suspicious object which they spotted was reported and, if a vehicle, its position and direction of travel was given. Army Air Corps Scout or RAF Wessex helicopters would then fly to the spot with troops to intercept.[19] The Scout general utility helicopter was also used for airborne patrols and for dropping soldiers to form surprise vehicle check points; and a helicopter could often be seen parked beside a road near the border while the soldiers it carried were stopping and checking civilian cars.

The Sioux acquired, as part of its equipment, a very powerful searchlight called a 'Night Sun Lamp'. The beam of this can be focused so that it can be spread wide to cover a considerable area, and then concentrated to a point to bear on a particular object. Strangely, the searchlight presents a very difficult target for a man on the ground to aim at.[20]

Bomb Disposal

The time bomb is a very favourite weapon of the IRA, particularly so when other means of aggression are being progressively denied to them. There have been many casualties amongst the very gallant bomb disposal teams of the Royal Army Ordnance Corps. A very effective equipment which has saved many lives was developed in 1973. The official title of this is the Remote Handling Equipment (Tracked) Explosive Ordnance Disposal, but it is more familiarly known as the 'Wheelbarrow'. It enables the operator to examine suspect items closely whilst remaining at a safe distance. It consists of a mobile tracked trolley connected by an electric cable to a remote control box. Its boom carries a television camera and a window breaker attachment. Other equipments, such as a rifle, can also be fitted. If it is desired to examine a suspect car, for instance, the trolley can be run up to it and a window smashed to enable the television attachment to have a look inside.[21]

The Royal Military Police

The Royal Military Police have a long and distinguished record in connection with the 'troubles' in Ireland, starting in the years following World War I when the Author's father was Provost Marshal and Commandant of the Corps. There was a very close collaboration with the Royal Irish Constabulary which has continued with their descendants, the Royal Ulster Constabulary. Now, for the first time in its history, the Corps has two regiments which are stationed in Northern Ireland and which have attached to them a WRAC Provost detachment. One company of a regiment is permanently in support of the RUC and there are frequently combined RMP and RUC patrols. On these duties the RMP normally wear service dress and their red cap to emphasise their police function. Another company provides escorts and bodyguards, and an investigations company looks into all shooting incidents in which military personnel are involved.[22]

Communications

The successful conduct of counter-insurgency operations depends to a great extent on rapid, reliable, and secure communications. This is the task, of course, of the Royal Signals. Every formation headquarters has its own signal unit. Headquarters Northern Ireland is served by No 233 Signal Squadron (NI) which is responsible for providing the communications from that headquarters to the three infantry brigades, to Great Britain, to the Northern Ireland Office at Stormont, and to all other important establishments in Northern Ireland. There is a radio relay trunk communication system providing secure voice channels through an automatic exchange and secure telegraph circuits. This ensures the continuance of reliable communications between all important points in the event of destruction by the IRA of Post Office lines and exchanges. There is also a system called Ulsternet which provides common user radio nets for a variety of purposes and covering the whole Province.

There are three other signal units, 3rd Infantry Brigade Headquarters and Signal Squadron, 8th Infantry Brigade Headquarters and Signal Squadron, and 39th Infantry Brigade Headquarters and Signal Squadron, each looking after the communication requirements of their own brigades. The 3rd Infantry Brigade's responsibilities cover the more southerly parts of Northern Ireland, the 8th Infantry Brigade has the City of Londonderry and the more northerly areas, whilst the 39th Brigade's area is the City of Belfast and a large part of County Antrim.[23]

Terrorist Weapons

A disturbing feature of the present insurgency is the ease with which the IRA and, indeed, the 'Loyalist' extremists have been able to acquire arms. The IRA, which in 1969 was relatively poorly armed, soon acquired large stocks from the USA, probably principally from the Irish-American community on the east coast. By 1970 they already had a considerable number of various types, amongst which the American M1 carbine seems to have been particularly popular.[24] It was accepted by the US Army in 1941 and more than $5\frac{1}{2}$ million carbines were made by a large number of manufacturers. It is a semi-automatic light rifle with a muzzle velocity of 1,950ft.[25] In 1972 Armalite rifles came into the possession of the IRA. The first Armalite rifle, the AR-10, was produced in 1955 by the Armalite Division of the Fairchild Engine and Airplane Company. It took the standard NATO 7.62mm ammunition. In 1959 the production of a scaled down version was licensed to Colt, and this was the AR-15 of 5.56mm calibre which is now, as the M16, the standard US Army rifle. It can fire either as a semi-automatic or an automatic. Several million have been made and are in use throughout the world. Following this, in the mid-1960s, the Armalite Company turned out a simpler, cheaper, and more rugged version, the AR-18, which is now made also in the United Kingdom by Sterling Armaments Ltd. It has not yet been accepted by the US Army. The sale of automatic weapons to the public is illegal in the USA so the AR-180 was produced as a non-automatic hunting rifle for civilian purchase. These weapons have the high muzzle velocity of 3,250fps.[26] The IRA had the AR-180 by 1972; it was of course easily purchasable in the United States. In 1973 the first AR-15 rifles were captured by the Security Forces.[27] A favourite sub-machine gun is the US M3, popularly known as the 'Grease Gun', a simple cheap weapon adopted by the US Army in 1942 and designed for mass production. It has a .45in calibre and the low muzzle velocity of 900fps.[28] The IRA have also a silenced version.[29]

The 'Loyalists' do not have a large sympathetic following in the United States, and most of the weapons of these extremists are old ones acquired in the past or newer ones stolen from the Security Forces. In addition, they have manufactured a number of sub-machine guns.[30]

Obviously, a major objective of the Security Forces is to stop the illegal import into Northern Ireland of weapons, ammunition and explosives; but success of course depends on effective measures being taken on both sides of the border.

Below left: A soldier of The King's Own Royal Border Regiment on patrol in the Protestant area of Belfast in 1974/75. Note the letters UVF (Ulster Volunteer Force) on the wall. / *Museum of The King's Own Royal Border Regiment*

Below: A soldier of The King's Own Border on patrol in the Lower Falls, Belfast, in 1974/75. / *Museum of The King's Own Royal Border Regiment*

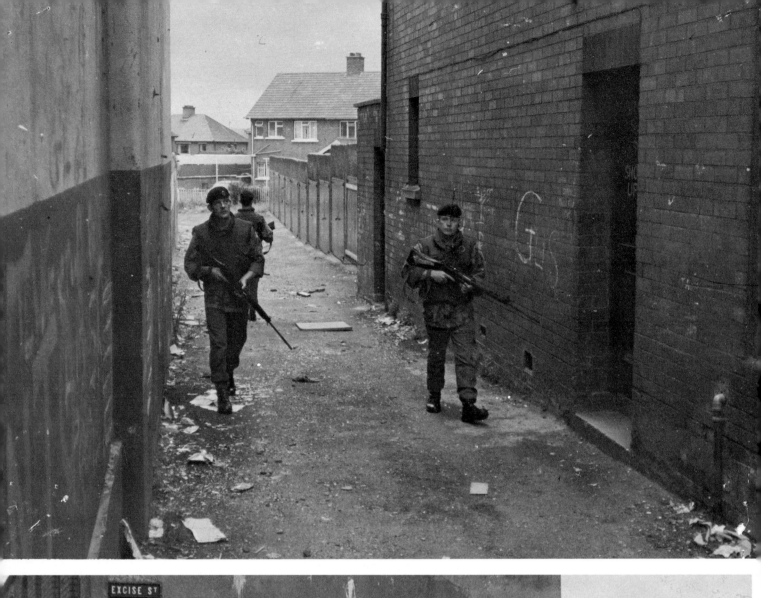

Left: **A King's Own Border patrol in Belfast 1976. Note the soldier in the background covering the entrance to the alleyway.** / *Museum of The King's Own Royal Border Regiment*

Below left: **The King's Own Border patrolling a distillery in Belfast 1974/75.** / *Museum of The King's Own Royal Border Regiment*

Top right: **A King's Own Border mobile patrol; Belfast 1976.** / *Museum of The King's Own Royal Border Regiment*

Centre right: **Another view of a mobile patrol: Belfast 1976.** / *Museum of The King's Own Royal Border Regiment*

Below: **Patrolling the Lower Falls, Belfast, in 1974/75. The soldier nearest the camera is covering the remainder of the patrol who are in the background.** / *Museum of The King's Own Royal Border Regiment*

Left: **Private Knight of The King's Own Royal Border Regiment on the alert.** / *Museum of The King's Own Royal Border Regiment*

Below left: **Ready for instant action; a soldier of The King's Own Border in Belfast 1974/75.** / *Museum of The King's Own Royal Border Regiment*

Top right: **Ready to give covering fire; a soldier of The King's Own Border with a 5.56mm Sterling Light Automatic Rifle. Belfast 1976.** / *Museum of The King's Own Royal Border Regiment*

Centre right: **Night patrol in Belfast 1974.** / *Museum of The King's Own Royal Border Regiment*

Below: **Soldiers clearing their weapons after returning from patrol. Belfast 1974/75.** / *Museum of The King's Own Royal Border Regiment*

Left: The operations officer in the operations room of the 1st Battalion The King's Own Royal Border Regiment; Belfast 1974/75. / *Museum of The King's Own Royal Border Regiment*

Below: A soldier of The King's Own Border wearing a combat helmet with visor at a chain barrier in Belfast, 1976. / *Museum of The King's Own Royal Border Regiment*

Right: A soldier on guard wearing combat helmet and visor; Belfast 1976. / *Museum of The King's Own Royal Border Regiment*

Below right: Soldiers alighting from a Saracen armoured personnel carrier. / *Crown Copyright*

Above: **A Shorland armoured car.**
/ *Crown Copyright*

Left: **A 'Wheelbarrow'.** / *Crown Copyright*

Right: The Wheelbarrow camera examining the inside of a suspect car after its window breaker attachment has smashed through a side window. / *Crown Copyright*

Below: A Wheelbarrow with rifle attachment after shooting open a suspect package attached to a railway wagon. / *Crown Copyright*

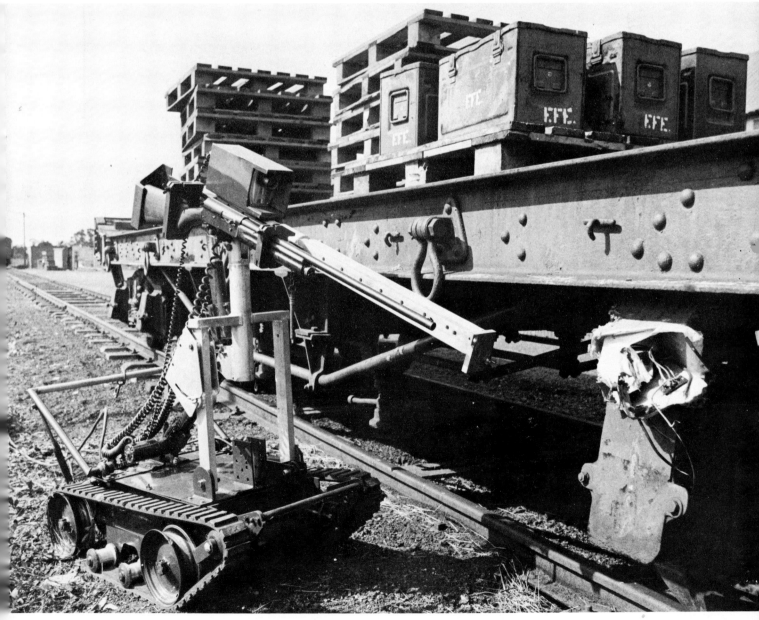

Peace and prosperity will no doubt return in due course to Northern Ireland, but when it does it will be due in large measure to the British Army and above all to the courage, discipline, morale, and good humour of that paragon amongst men — the British Soldier.

Below: Lieutenant David Keith commanding his platoon of The Gordon Highlanders during an incident following the Queen's visit to Northern Ireland in 1977. A photograph taken by Captain A. J. Tait, The Gordon Highlanders. / *Crown Copyright*

Notes to the Text

Chapter 1

1 Captain H. M. McCance; 'Uniforms of the British Army: Red Coat under Fire', *Journal of the Society for Army Historical Research* vol XIV (1933); p62
2 Colonel H. C. B. Rogers; *Weapons of the British Soldier*; London, Seeley Service, 1960; pp245-8
   Ian V. Hogg & John Weeks; *Military Small Arms of the 20th Century*; London, Arms & Armour Press, 1977; pp113, 118
3 ibid p220
4 *Black & White Budget*; London, The Black & White Publishing Co, 1900; Parts 20 and 25
5 David James; *Lord Roberts*; London, Hollis & Carter, 1954; p346
6 B. H. Liddell Hart; *History of the First World War*; London, Cassell, 1970; p61
7 *Black & White Budget*; op cit Parts 3, 14, 15
   Treatise on Military Carriages; Prepared in the Carriage Branch, Ordnance College; 7th edn, London, 1911; pp198-9, 209
8 Major-General J. F. C. Fuller; *The Conduct of War*; London, Eyre & Spottiswoode, 1961; pp128-130
9 ibid pp156-8
10 Liddell Hart, op cit p57
11 ibid pp175, 177
12 Hogg & Weeks, op cit pp222-3
13 M. M. Postan; 'British War Production', *History of the Second World War*; London, HM Stationery Office, 1952; p27
14 ibid p6
15 ibid p7
   Hogg & Weeks, op cit p229
16 Rogers, op cit p249
17 Major L. F. Ellis; 'The War in France and Flanders, 1939-1940', *History of the Second World War*; London, HM Stationery Office, 1953; pp358f
18 ibid pp159, 168
19 ibid p326
20 Major A. T. H. Durand & Major R. H. W. S. Hastings; *The London Rifle Brigade, 1919-1950*; Aldershot, Gale & Polden, 1952; p132
21 Brigadier Norman Skentlebury; *Arrows to Atom Bombs: A History of the Ordnance Board*; London, HMSO, 1975; pp83-5
22 Brigadier C. N. Barclay; 'The British Regimental System', *Brassey's Annual, 1972;* London, William Clowes, 1972; p133

Chapter 2

1 Colonel H. C. B. Rogers; *The Mounted Troops of the British Army*; 2nd edn, London, Seeley Service, 1967; pp230-1
2 ibid pp213-4
3 Ian V. Hogg & John Weeks; *Military Small Arms of the 20th Century*; London, Arms & Armour Press, 1977; p118
4 Colonel H. C. B. Rogers; *Tanks in Battle*; London, Seeley Service, 1965; pp40, 42, 44, 63, 68-9

5 Rogers; *Mounted Troops*; op cit p241
6 M. M. Postan; 'British War Production', *History of the Second World War*; London, HM Stationery Office, 1952; p7
7 Rogers; *Tanks in Battle*; op cit pp63, 66-7
8 ibid pp77-79
9 ibid p82
10 ibid pp85, 95
11 ibid p87
12 ibid p90
13 ibid p96
14 ibid pp100, 109, 99
   Hogg & Weeks, op cit p230
15 Rogers; *Tanks in Battle*; op cit pp100-112
16 Rogers; *Mounted Troops*; op cit pp246-7
17 Rogers; *Tanks in Battle*; op cit pp114-5
18 ibid pp100-101, 128
19 ibid p101
20 ibid p133
21 ibid p148
22 ibid p171
23 ibid p175
24 ibid pp183-4
25 ibid pp197-9
26 ibid p200
27 ibid pp216-9

Chapter 3

1 Major-General J. F. C. Fuller; *The Conduct of War*; London, Eyre & Spottiswoode, 1961; pp134-140
   Colonel H. C. B. Rogers; *Artillery through the Ages*; London, Seeley Service, 1971; pp113f
2 ibid p116
3 ibid pp113-4
4 ibid pp119-122
5 ibid p120
6 *Black & White Budget*; London, W. J. P. Moncton, 1899-1900; Part 11, p9
7 Rogers, op cit pp122-4
8 ibid pp127-8, 157
9 ibid p133
10 ibid p135
   Brigadier Norman Skentlebury; *Arrows to Atom Bombs*; London, HM Stationery Office, 1975; p31
11 ibid pp65-6
   Rogers, op cit p159
12 ibid pp158-160, 176
   Skentlebury, op cit pp65-6
13 Rogers, op cit pp169-170
14 ibid pp170-1
15 ibid pp172-4
   Skentlebury, op cit pp69-72

16 Rogers, op cit pp181-3
17 ibid p184

Chapter 4

1 Derek Boyd; *Royal Engineers*; London, Leo Cooper, 1975; pp65-7
2 *Documents Relating to the Naval Air Service*; vol I 1908-1918, ed Captain S. W. Roskill; Navy Records Society, 1969; pp25-6
3 Boyd, op cit pp71-83
4 *Military Operations France and Belgium 1918*; vol IV, ed Brigadier-General Sir James Edmonds; London, HM Stationery Office, 1947; pp23-4
5 Boyd, op cit pp71-83
6 ibid
7 ibid
8 ibid pp83-5
9 ibid
10 ibid pp89-95
    Colonel H. C. B. Rogers; *The Last Steam Locomotive Engineer: R. A. Riddles, CBE*; London, George Allen & Unwin, 1970; pp109-110
11 Boyd, op cit pp89-96
12 ibid pp96-97
13 ibid pp89-95
14 ibid pp108-9
15 ibid pp121-2
    Major-General J. L. Moulton; *Battle for Antwerp*; London, Ian Allan Ltd, 1978; p203
16 ibid pp77, 204
17 ibid pp91-5
18 ibid p143

Chapter 5

1 Major-General R. F. H. Nalder; *The Royal Corps of Signals*; London, Royal Signals Institution, 1958; p19
2 ibid pp40-46
3 ibid pp40-46
4 ibid pp50-53
5 ibid p77
6 ibid pp97-100
7 ibid pp106-7
8 ibid p108
9 ibid pp191-3
10 ibid p105
11 ibid p123
12 ibid p143
13 ibid p241
14 ibid p254
15 I Corinthians, 15:33

Chapter 6

For the information contained in this Chapter I am indebted to Major-General Sir Cecil Smith, KBE, MC, late Colonel Commandant of the Royal Corps of Transport.

Chapter 7

1 H. M. Chichester & G. Burgess-Short; *The Records and Badges of Every Regiment and Corps in the British Army*; 2nd edn, London, Gale & Polden, 1900; p924
2 ibid pp931-2
    Brigadier A. H. Fernyhough; *History of the Royal Army Ordnance Corps 1920-1945*; Royal Army Ordnance Corps, 1967; ppix-x
3 Major D. E. King; 'The Survival of Tanks in Battle; *Journal of the Royal United Services Institute*; vol 123, 1978; p26-7
4 Fernyhough, op cit ppix-x
5 ibid pp3-4
6 ibid pp4-5
7 ibid p15
8 ibid p34
9 ibid p54
10 ibid p63
11 ibid p67
12 King, op cit p27
13 Fernyhough, op cit pp79-81
14 King, op cit p27

15 Fernyhough, op cit p90
16 ibid pp117-119
17 King, op cit p27
18 Captain D. E. King; 'Repairing AFVs in Battle', *British Army Review*; No 12, April 1976
19 Fernyhough, op cit, pp167, 380
20 King; 'The Survival of Tanks in Battle'; op cit p28
21 King; 'Repairing AFVs in Battle'; op cit p41

Chapter 8

1 I. V. Hogg & J. Weeks; *Military Small Arms of the 20th Century*; London, Arms & Armour Press, 1977; pp20, 147, 198, 235
2 J. Weeks; 'The British 4.85 Weapon System', *Guns Review*; August 1976
3 *RSAF Enfield, 4.85 Weapon System*; RSAF Leaflet
    RUSI & Brassey's Defence Yearbook 1977/78, 'Army Weapons'; London, Brassey's Publishers, 1977; pp264f
    Hogg & Weeks; op cit pp163-6, 235-6
4 *81mm The British Lightweight Mortar*; Ministry of Defence Pamphlet
5 *51mm Mortar*; Ministry of Defence Leaflet
6 *Jane's Weapons Systems*, 1978; ed R. T. Pretty; London, Macdonald & Jane's, 1977
7 ibid
    RUSI & Brassey's, op cit
8 *Jane's Weapon Systems*, op cit p444
    Brassey's Annual 1970, 'Developments in Army Equipment'; Brigadier P. H. C. Hayward; London, William Clowes, 1970; pp262-3
9 *Brassey's 1970*; op cit p254
10 *RUSI & Brassey's 1977/78*, op cit p277
    Brigadier N. Skentlebury; *Arrows to Atom Bombs*; London, HM Stationery Office, 1975; pp113-4
11 *Rarden 30mm Self Loading Gun*; Ministry of Defence Pamphlet
    Jane's Weapon Systems, op cit p402
    Colonel N. L. Dodd; 'The Day of the Scorpion', *The Army Quarterly*; vol 107 (October 1977); p439
12 *Jane's Weapon Systems*, op cit p381
    Brassey's Annual 1972, 'Developments in the Weapons and Equipment of Land Warfare'; Brigadier P. H. C. Hayward; London, William Clowes, 1972; p279
13 *105mm Light Gun*; Ministry of Defence Pamphlet
    Jane's Weapon Systems, op cit p400
    Brassey's Annual 1971, 'Land Warfare Equipment'; Brigadier P. H. C. Haywards; London, William Clowes, 1971; pp260-2
    Brassey's 1972, op cit p279
14 Skentlebury, op cit p82
15 *Jane's Weapon Systems*, op cit p399
    Brassey's Annual 1971, op cit pp259-260
16 Skentlebury, op cit p3
    Brassey's 1977/78, op cit p295
    Jane's Weapon Systems, op cit p378
17 ibid p407
18 ibid p405
    Brassey's 1977/78, op cit pp300-301
19 ibid
    Skentlebury, op cit p82
    Jane's Weapon Systems, op cit p406
20 ibid pp387, 404
    Brassey's 1977/78, op cit p303
21 Skentlebury, op cit pp72-3
22 *Jane's Weapon Systems*, op cit p402
23 ibid
24 *Brassey's 1977/78*, op cit pp282-4
25 ibid p285
    Jane's Weapon Systems, op cit p40
    RUSI Seminar 10 December 1975, *Tactical Employment and Comparative Performance of Ground and Air-Launched Anti-Tank Weapons*
26 *Jane's Weapon Systems*, op cit p41
27 ibid p36
    RUSI Seminar, op cit
    Brassey's 1977/78, op cit pp288-9
    Major P. H. Ll. Hirsch; 'What is Milan ?', *British Army Review*; No 53, August 1976

28 *Jane's Weapon Systems*, op cit p96
   Brassey's 1970, op cit p266
29 *Jane's Weapon Systems*, op cit p81
   John Marriott; 'Air Defence of Units in the Field', *The Army Quarterly*; vol 18, (January 1978); pp21-3
30 *Brassey's 1977/78*, pp284-5
   RUSI Seminar, op cit
   Jane's Weapon Systems, op cit pp44, 159
31 *RUSI and Brassey's Defence Yearbook 1974*, 'Tactical or Battlefield Nuclear Weapons'; London, Brassey's Naval & Shipping Annual, 1974; pp222-3
   Brassey's 1977/78, op cit pp264-5
   Jane's Weapon Systems, op cit p51
32 *British Bar Mine System*; Ministry of Defence Pamphlet
   Brassey's 1970, op cit pp253-4
33 *Ranger*; (EMI Electronics Pamphlet)
34 *Giant Viper*; Ministry of Defence Pamphlet
35 *Brassey's 1977/78*, op cit pp267-8

Chapter 9

1 *RUSI & Brassey's Defence Yearbook 1977/78*, 'Army Weapons'; London, Brassey's Publishers, 1977; pp271-282
2 *Jane's Weapon Systems, 1978*; London, Macdonald & Jane's, 1977; pp340-1
   Brassey's Annual 1970, 'Developments in Army Equipment'; Brigadier P. H. C. Hayward; London, William Clowes, 1970; pp255-8
   Brassey's Annual 1972, 'Developments in Weapons and Equipment of Land Warfare'; Brigadier P. H. C. Hayward; London, William Clowes, 1972; pp271-3
   The Future of the Battle Tank in a European Conflict; Seminar held at the RUSI 20 March 1974
3 ibid
4 Colonel N. L. Dodd; 'The Day of the Scorpion'; *The Army Quarterly*; vol 107 (October 1977); p438
   Scorpion; Alvis Ltd
5 Dodd, op cit
   Scimitar; Alvis Ltd
6 Dodd, op cit
   Striker; Alvis Ltd
7 Dodd, ob cit
   Spartan; Alvis Ltd
8 Dodd, op cit
   Sultan; Alvis Ltd
9 Dodd, op cit
   Samson; Alvis Ltd
10 Dodd, op cit
   Samaritan; Alvis Ltd
11 *Fox*; Ministry of Defence pamphlet
12 *Jane's Weapon Systems*, op cit p347
13 ibid p341

Chapter 10

1 Lieutenant-General Sir Napier Crookenden, at the RUSI Seminar 1971
2 *Brassey's Annual 1971*, 'The Helicopter and Land Warfare'; Lieutenant-Colonel H. P. Trueman; London, William Clowes, 1971
3 RUSI Seminar 1971; *The Role of the Helicopter in the Land Battle*
4 ibid
   Brassey's 1971, op cit
5 RUSI Seminar, op cit
6 *Brassey's Annual 1973*, 'Developments in Land Warfare'; Brigadier P. H. C. Hayward; London, William Clowes, 1973
   Jane's Weapon Systems, 1978; London, Macdonald & Jane's 1977; p94
7 Lieutenant-Colonel J. E. Evererett-Heath; 'Attack Helicopters Advance', *British Army Review*; No 57, December 1977
8 Lieutenant-Colonel A. C. Uloth; 'He who Fights', *British Army Review*; No 51, December 1975
9 RUSI Seminar, op cit
   HQ Director Army Air Corps
10 ibid
   RUSI Seminar, op cit
11 ibid

12 Dr D. Chaplin; 'MDH and the Armed Helicopters', *British Army Review*; No 49, April 1975
13 RUSI Seminar, op cit
14 Uloth, op cit
15 *Brassey's Annual 1970*, 'The Operational Employment of the Harrier'; Air Vice-Marshal P. de L. le Cheminant; London, William Clowes, 1970
16 RUSI Seminar, op cit
17 ibid
18 *RUSI & Brassey's Defence Yearbook 1977/8*, 'Army Weapons'; London, Brassey's Publishers, 1977; p287
   RUSI Seminar, op cit
   Uloth, op cit
   AAC, op cit
19 ibid
   Uloth, op cit
20 RUSI Seminar, op cit
21 Frank Kitson; 'The New British Armoured Division', *RUSI Journal*; March 1977
   Flight International, 2 July 1977, 'World Air Forces 1977', p47
   AAC, op cit

Chapter 11

1 *RUSI & Brassey's Defence Yearbook 1977/78*, 'Army Weapons'; London, Brassey's Publishers, 1977; pp326-331
2 ibid
   Brassey's Annual 1971, 'Land Warfare Equipment'; Brigadier P. H. C. Hayward; London, William Clowes, 1971
3 *British Army Equipment Exhibition Catalogue* 19-23 June 1978; pp162-3, 180-1
4 *Brassey's 1977/78*, op cit
5 ibid
6 ibid
7 ibid
8 ibid
9 *Brassey's 1974*, op cit
10 *Ferranti Ltd*; (Brochure)
11 *Brassey's 1974*, op cit
12 ibid
   Brassey's 1977/78, op cit
13 ibid
14 *Brassey's 1974*, op cit
15 *Brassey's 1977/78*, op cit

Chapter 12

1 *Brassey's Annual 1971*, 'Land Warfare Equipment'; Brigadier P. H. C. Hayward; London, William Clowes, 1971
   British Army Equipment Exhibition 19-23 June 1978; Catalogue, p82
2 *Brassey's 1971*, op cit
3 ibid
   British Army Equipment, op cit p138
4 Ministry of Defence
5 ibid
6 British Army Equipment, op cit p141
7 Ministry of Defence
8 British Army Equipment, op cit pp18, 90
9 Ministry of Defence
10 ibid
   British Military Vehicles 1971; The Military Vehicles and Engineering Establishment; p96
11 ibid p28
12 *Soldier*; July 1978
13 ibid April 1978, August 1978
14 Ministry of Defence
15 General Sir John Hackett and others; *The Third World War*; London, Sidgwick & Jackson, 1978; pp149-150, 164-166

Chapter 13

1 General Sir John Hackett; *The Third World War*; London, Sidgwick & Jackson, 1978; p127
2 'The Readiness of AMF'; *Soldier*; November 1978
3 Ministry of Defence
4 ibid
5 ibid

6   'Reserve Forces', *A seminar at the Royal United Services Institute*; *RUSI Journal*; September 1978
7   Ministry of Defence
8   'Reserve Forces', op cit

Chapter 14

1   Frank Kitson; 'The New British Armoured Division', *RUSI Journal*; March 1977
2   Ministry of Defence
3   Colonel H. C. B. Rogers; *Napoleon's Army*; London, Ian Allan Ltd, 1974; pp138-145
4   Brigadier H. B. C. Watkins; 'The Indispensable Scout', *Armor*; vol LXXXVII No 4 (1976)
5   Major M. H. G. Young; 'Bulk Fuel and the Central Pipeline System', *British Army Review*; No 56, August 1977
6   Colonel J. D. Bastick; 'Logistic Support in War', *British Army Review*; No 59, August 1978
7   Editorial, *British Army Review*; No 55, April 1977
8   Captain M. R. Fredericks; 'Tug of War', *British Army Review*; No 57, December 1977
9   *Brassey's Annual 1973*, 'Close Air Support for NATO'; Wing-Commander D. C. G. Brook; London, William Clowes, 1973
10 *Brassey's Annual 1970*, 'The Operational Employment of Harrier'; Air Vice-Marshal P. de L. Le Cheminant; London, William Clowes, 1970

Chapter 15

1   General Sir John Hackett; *The Third World War*; London, Sidgwick & Jackson, 1978; p156
2   ibid p127
3   ibid p152
4   ibid pp128, 154
5   ibid pp129-131
6   ibid pp151-2
7   General Carl von Clausewitz; *On War*; tr Colonel J. J. Graham, 1873, vol I; London, Routledge & Keegan Paul, new edition; pp77-9
8   Editorial, *British Army Review*; No 55, April 1977
9   *RUSI & Brassey's Defence Yearbook 1974*, 'Reflections on the Middle East War 6-24 October 1973'; Stewart Menaul; London, Brassey's Naval & Shipping Annual, 1974
10 Ministry of Defence
11 Hackett, op cit
12 'KAR'; 'A Personal View of the Yom Kippur War', *British Army Review*; No 50, August 1975
    Jac Weller; 'APCs in the Yom Kippur War', *British Army Review*; No 49, April 1975
13 'KAR', op cit
14 Jac Weller, op cit
15 'KAR', op cit
16 ibid
17 ibid
18 Comte de Saxe; *Mes Réveries*; ed M. l'Abbe Perau; Amsterdam, Arkstée et Markus, 1757); vol II pp142-150 (Passage tr by Colonel H. C. B. Rogers)

19 Clausewitz, op cit p82
20 Christopher Donnelly; 'The Soviet Soldier', *British Army Review*; No 55, April 1977
21 Information to Author

Chapter 16

1   W. Moore; 'The Ulster Defence Regiment', *British Army Review*; No 56, August 1977
    Brassey's Annual 1973, 'Northern Ireland to 1973'; Brigadier W. F. K. Thompson; London, William Clowes, 1973
2   ibid
3   Frank Kitson; *Low Intensity Operations*; London, Faber & Faber, 1972; p90
4   Moore, op cit
    David Barzilay; *The British Army in Ulster*; vol 1, Belfast, Century Books, 1973; pp153-6
5   Moore, op cit
6   ibid
    Barzilay, op cit
7   Moore, op cit
8   ibid
9   'A Greenfinch'; 'Women of the UDR', *British Army Review*; No 56, December 1975
10 Barzilay, op cit vol 2 (1975), pp65-80
11 Thompson, op cit
12 *Brassey's Annual 1972*, 'The Army in Northern Ireland'; Michael Banks; London, William Clowes, 1972
    Barzilay, op cit, vol I p71
13 Thompson, op cit
14 *British Military Vehicles 1971*; The Military Vehicles and Engineering Establishment; pp140-1
    Jane's Weapon Systems, 1978; ed R. T. Pretty; London, Macdonald & Jane's, 1977; p348
15 Staff Sergeant R. D. Jones; 'Terrorist Weaponry in Northern Ireland', *British Army Review*; No 58, April 1978
16 *Jane's Weapon Systems*, op cit p345
17 Barzilay, op cit vol 1, pp153-7
18 *Jane's Weapon Systems*, op cit, pp346-7
    Brassey's Annual, 'Land Warfare Equipment'; Brigadier P. H. C. Hayward; London, William Clowes, 1971
19 Barzilay, op cit vol 1, pp137-8
20 ibid pp173-9
21 Ministry of Defence Leaflet
22 Barzilay, op cit vol 1, pp187-9
23 ibid, vol 2, pp82-6
24 Jones, op cit
25 Ian V. Hogg and John Weeks; *Military Small Arms of the 20th Century*; London, Arms and Armour Press, 1977; pp184-5
26 ibid pp186-190
27 Jones, op cit
28 Hogg & Weeks, op cit p102
29 Jones, op cit
30 ibid

Appendix

The Regiments and Corps of the British Army

(Note: *Where 'The' with a capital 'T' precedes a regimental title, it forms part of that title*)

Household Cavalry

1 *The Life Guards*
In April 1922 The First Life Guards and The 2nd Life Guards amalgamated to form The Life Guards (1st and 2nd). In June 1928 the Regiment was redesignated The Life Guards.
2 *The Blues and Royals* (Royal Horse Guards and 1st Dragoons)
On 29 March 1969 The Royal Horse Guards (The Blues) and The Royal Dragoons (1st Dragoons) amalgamated with the above title.

Royal Armoured Corps

1 *1st The Queen's Dragoon Guards*
On 1 January 1959, 1st King's Dragoon Guards and The Queen's Bays (2nd Dragoon Guards) amalgamated with the above title.
2 *The Royal Scots Dragoon Guards* (Carabiniers and Greys)
On 11 April 1922, 3rd Dragoon Guards (Prince of Wales's) and The Carabiniers (6th Dragoon Guards) amalgamated to form 3rd/6th Dragoon Guards. On 31 December 1928 the Regiment was redesignated 3rd Carabiniers (Prince of Wales's Dragoon Guards). On 2 July 1971 The Royal Scots Greys (2nd Dragoons) and 3rd Carabiniers (Prince of Wales's Dragoon Guards) amalgamated as The Royal Scots Dragoon Guards (Carabiniers and Greys).
3 *4th/7th Royal Dragoon Guards*
On 11 April 1922, 4th Royal Irish Dragoon Guards and 7th Dragoon Guards (Princess Royal's) amalgamated to form 4th/7th Dragoon Guards. On 31 October 1936 the Regiment was redesignated 4th/7th Royal Dragoon Guards.
4 *5th Royal Inniskilling Dragoon Guards*
On 11 April 1922, 5th Dragoon Guards (Princess Charlotte of Wales's) and The Inniskillings (6th Dragoons) amalgamated as 5th/6th Dragoons. On 31 May 1927 the Regiment was redesignated 5th Inniskilling Dragoon Guards, and on 30 June 1935 this was changed to 5th Royal Inniskilling Dragoon Guards.
5 *The Queen's Own Hussars*
On 3 November 1958, 3rd The King's Own Hussars and 7th Queen's Own Hussars amalgamated with the above title.
6 *The Queen's Royal Irish Hussars*
On 24 October 1958, 4th Queen's Own Hussars and 8th King's Royal Irish Hussars amalgamated with the above title.
7 *9th/12th Royal Lancers (Prince of Wales's)*
On 11 September 1960, 9th Queen's Royal Lancers and 12th Royal Lancers (Prince of Wales's) amalgamated with the above title.
8 *The Royal Hussars (Prince of Wales's Own)*
On 25 October 1969, 10th Royal Hussars (Prince of Wales's Own) and 11th Hussars (Prince Albert's Own) amalgamated with the above title.
9 *13th/18th Royal Hussars (Queen Mary's Own)*
On 11 April 1922, 13th Hussars and 18th Royal Hussars (Queen Mary's Own) amalgamated as 13th/18th Hussars. On 31 December 1935 the title was changed to 13th/18th Royal Hussars (Queen Mary's Own).
10 *14th/20th King's Hussars*
On 11 April 1922, 14th King's Hussars and 20th Hussars amalgamated as 14th/20th Hussars. On 31 December 1936 this was changed to 14th/20th King's Hussars.
11 *15th/19th The King's Royal Hussars*
On 11 April 1922, 15th The King's Hussars and 19th Royal Hussars (Queen Alexandra's Own) amalgamated as 15th/19th Hussars. On 31 October 1932 the Regiment was redesignated 15th The King's Royal Hussars, and on 31 December 1933 this was changed to 15th/19th The King's Royal Hussars.
12 *16th/5th The Queen's Royal Lancers*
On 11 April 1922, 15th The Queen's Lancers and 5th Royal Irish Lancers amalgamated as 16th/5th Lancers. On 16 June 1954 the Regiment was redesignated 16th/5th The Queen's Royal Lancers.
13 *17th/21st Lancers*
On 11 April 1922, 17th Lancers (Duke of Cambridge's Own) and 21st Lancers (Empress of India's) amalgamated with the above title.
14 *Royal Tank Regiment*
On 28 July 1917 the Tank Corps was formed from the Heavy Branch of the Machine Gun Corps. On 18 October 1923 the Corps was redesignated Royal Tank Corps, and on 4 April 1939 this became Royal Tank Regiment.

Royal Armoured Corps TAVR

1 *The Royal Yeomanry*
Squadron titles: Royal Wiltshire Yeomanry, Sherwood Rangers Yeomanry, Kent and County of London Yeomanry, North Irish Horse, and Berkshire and Westminster Dragoons.
2 *The Wessex Yeomanry*
Squadron titles: Royal Wiltshire Yeomanry, Royal Gloucestershire Hussars, and Royal Devon Yeomanry.
3 *The Queen's Own Yeomanry*
Squadron titles: Queen's Own Yorkshire Yeomanry, Ayrshire Yeomanry, Cheshire Yeomanry, and Northumberland Hussars.
4 *The Duke of Lancaster's Own Yeomanry*
Royal Regiment of Artillery
Royal Regiment of Artillery TAVR
The Honourable Artillery Company TAVR
Corps of Royal Engineers
Royal Monmouthshire Royal Engineers (Militia) TAVR
Corps of Royal Engineers TAVR
Corps of Royal Engineers TAVR, Postal and Courier Section
Corps of Royal Engineers TAVR, Engineer and Railway Staff Corps
Royal Corps of Signals
Royal Corps of Signals TAVR

The Guards Division

1 *Grenadier Guards* (two battalions)
2 *Coldstream Guards* (two battalions
3 *Scots Guards* (two battalions)
4 *Irish Guards* (one battalion)
5 *Welsh Guards* (one battalion)

The Scottish Division

1 *The Royal Scots (The Royal Regiment)* (1) (one battalion)
2 *The Royal Highland Fusiliers (Princess Margaret's Own Glasgow and Ayrshire Regiment)* (21, 71, and 74) (one battalion)
On 20 January 1959, The Royal Scots Fusiliers (21) and The Highland Light Infantry (City of Glasgow Regiment) (71 and 74) amalgamated with the above title.
3 *The King's Own Scottish Borderers* (25) (one battalion)

4 *The Black Watch (Royal Highland Regiment)* (42 and 73) (one battalion)
5 *Queen's Own Highlanders (Seaforth and Camerons)* (72, 78, and 79) (one battalion)
On 7 February 1961 the Seaforth Highlanders (Ross-shire Buffs, The Duke of Albany's) (72 and 78) and The Queen's Own Cameron Highlanders (79) amalgamated with the above title.
6 *The Gordon Highlanders* (75 and 92) (one battalion)
7 *The Argyll and Sutherland Highlanders (Princess Louise's)* (91 and 93 (one battalion)

The Scottish Division TAVR

1 *1st Battalion 52nd Lowland Volunteers*
2 *2nd Battalion 52nd Lowland Volunteers*
3 *1st Battalion 51st Highland Volunteers*
4 *2nd Battalion 51st Highland Volunteers*
5 *3rd Battalion 51st Highland Volunteers*

The Queen's Division

1 *The Queen's Regiment* (2, 3, 31, 35, 50, 57, 70, 77, 97, 107) (three battalions)
On 14 October 1959 The Queen's Royal Regiment (West Surrey) (2) and The East Surrey Regiment (31 and 70) amalgamated as The Queen's Royal Surrey Regiment. On 1 March 1961 The Buffs (Royal East Kent Regiment) (3) and The Queen's Own Royal West Kent Regiment (50 and 97) amalgamated to form The Queen's Own Buffs The Royal Kent Regiment. On 31 December 1966 The Queen's Royal Surrey Regiment, The Queen's Own Buffs The Royal Kent Regiment, The Royal Sussex Regiment (35 and 107), and The Middlesex Regiment (Duke of Cambridge's Own (57 and 77) amalgamated as The Queen's Regiment.
2 *The Royal Regiment of Fusiliers* (5, 6, 7, and 20) (three battalions)
On 23 April 1968 The Royal Northumberland Fusiliers (5), The Royal Warwickshire Fusiliers (6), The Royal Fusiliers (City of London Regiment) (7), and The Lancashire Fusiliers (20) amalgamated to form The Royal Regiment of Fusiliers.
3 *The Royal Anglian Regiment* (9, 10, 12, 16, 17, 44, 48, 56 and 58) (three battalions)
On 2 June 1958 The Bedfordshire and Hertfordshire Regiment (16) and The Essex Regiment (44 and 56) amalgamated as The 3rd East Anglian Regiment (16th/44th Foot). On 29 August 1959 The Royal Norfolk Regiment (9) and The Suffolk Regiment (12) amalgamated to form The 1st East Anglian Regiment (Royal Norfolk and Suffolk). On 1 June 1960 The Royal Lincolnshire Regiment (10) and The Northamptonshire Regiment (48 and 58) amalgamated as the 2nd East Anglian Regiment (Duchess of Gloucester's Own Royal Lincolnshire and Northamptonshire). On 1 September 1964 the above regiments, together with The Royal Leicestershire Regiment (17) amalgamated as The Royal Anglian Regiment.

The Queen's Division TAVR

1 *5th (Volunteer) Battalion The Queen's Regiment*
2 *6th/7th (Volunteer) Battalion The Queen's Regiment*
3 *5th (Volunteer) Battalion The Royal Regiment of Fusiliers*
4 *6th (Volunteer) Battalion The Royal Regiment of Fusiliers*
5 *5th (Volunteer) Battalion The Royal Anglian Regiment*
6 *6th (Volunteer) Battalion The Royal Anglian Regiment*
7 *7th (Volunteer) Battalion The Royal Anglian Regiment*

The King's Division

1 *The King's Own Royal Border Regiment* (4, 34, and 55) (one battalion)
On 1 October 1959 The King's Own Royal Regiment (Lancaster) (4) and The Border Regiment (34 and 55) amalgamated as The King's Own Royal Border Regiment.
2 *The King's Regiment* (8, 63, and 96) (one battalion)
On 1 September 1958 The King's Regiment (Liverpool) (8) and The Manchester Regiment (63 and 96) amalgamated as The King's Regiment (Manchester and Liverpool). On 13 December 1968 this was changed to The King's Regiment.
3 *The Prince of Wales's Own Regiment of Yorkshire* (14 and 15) (one battalion)
On 25 April 1958 The West Yorkshire Regiment (The Prince of Wales's Own) (14) and The East Yorkshire Regiment (Duke of York's Own) (15) amalgamated with the above title.
4 *The Green Howards (Alexandra, Princess of Wales's Own Yorkshire Regiment)* (19) (one battalion)

5 *The Royal Irish Rangers* (27th [Inniskilling], 83rd and 87th) (two battalions)
On 1 July 1968 The Royal Inniskilling Fusiliers (27 and 108), The Royal Ulster Rifles (83 and 86) and The Royal Irish Fusiliers (Princess Victoria's) (87 and 89) amalgamated with the above title.
6 *The Queen's Lancashire Regiment* (30, 40, 47, 59, 81, and 82) (one battalion)
On 1 July 1958 The East Lancashire Regiment (30 and 59) and The South Lancashire Regiment (The Prince of Wales's Volunteers) (40 and 82) amalgamated as The Lancashire Regiment (Prince of Wales's Volunteers). On 25 March 1970 The Lancashire Regiment (Prince of Wales's Volunteers) amalgamated with The Loyal Regiment (North Lancashire) as The Queen's Lancashire Regiment.
7 *The Duke of Wellington's Regiment (West Riding)* (33 and 76) (one battalion)

The King's Division TAVR

1 4th (Volunteer) Battalion *The King's Own Royal Border Regiment*
2 5th/8th (Volunteer) Battalion *The Queen's Lancashire Regiment*
3 1st Battalion *Yorkshire Volunteers*
4 2nd Battalion *Yorkshire Volunteers*
5 3rd Battalion *Yorkshire Volunteers*
6 *The North Irish Horse Militia* (4th [Volunteer] Battalion The Royal Irish Rangers) (27th [Inniskilling] 83rd and 87th)
7. 5th (Volunteer) Battalion *The Royal Irish Rangers* (27th [Inniskilling] 83rd and 87th)

The Prince of Wales's Division

1 *The Devonshire and Dorset Regiment* (11, 39, and 54) (one battalion)
On 17 May 1958 The Devonshire Regiment (11) and The Dorset Regiment amalgamated with the above title.
2 *The Cheshire Regiment* (22) (one battalion)
3 *The Royal Welch Fusiliers* (23) (one battalion)
4 *The Royal Regiment of Wales* (24th/41st Foot) (one battalion)
On 11 June 1959 The South Wales Borderers (24) and The Welch Regiment (41 and 69) amalgamated under the above title.
5 *The Gloucestershire Regiment* (28 and 61) (one battalion)
6 *The Worcestershire and Sherwood Foresters Regiment (29th/45th Foot)* (29, 36, 45, and 95) (one battalion)
On 28 February 1970 The Worcestershire Regiment (29 and 36) and The Sherwood Foresters (Nottinghamshire and Derbyshire Regiment) (45 and 95) amalgamated with the above title.
7 *The Royal Hampshire Regiment (37 and 67)* (one battalion)
8 *The Staffordshire Regiment (The Princes of Wales's)* (38, 64, 80 and 98) (one battalion)
On 31 January 1959 The South Staffordshire Regiment (38 and 80) and The North Staffordshire Regiment (The Prince of Wales's) (64 and 98) amalgamated to form The Staffordshire Regiment (The Prince of Wales's).
9 *The Duke of Edinburgh's Royal Regiment (Berkshire and Wiltshire)* (49, 62, 66, and 99) (one battalion)
On 9 June 1959 The Royal Berkshire Regiment (Princess Charlotte of Wales's) (49 and 66) and the Wiltshire Regiment (Duke of Edinburgh's) (62 and 99) amalgamated under the above title.

The Prince of Wales's Division TAVR

1 *1st Battalion The Wessex Regiment (Rifle Volunteers)*
2 *2nd Battalion The Wessex Regiment (Volunteers)*
3 *1st Battalion Mercian Volunteers*
4 *2nd Battalion Mercian Volunteers*
5 *3rd (Volunteer) Battalion The Royal Welch Fusiliers*
6 *3rd (Volunteer) Battalion The Royal Regiment of Wales (24th/41st Foot)*
7 *4th (Volunteer) Battalion The Royal Regiment of Wales (24th/41st Foot)*
8 *3rd (Volunteer) Battalion The Worcestershire and Sherwood Foresters Regiment* (29th/45th Foot)

The Light Division

1 *The Light Infantry* (13, 32, 46, 51, 53, 68, 85, 105, 106) (three battalions)
On 6 October 1959 The Somerset Light Infantry (Prince Albert's) (13) and The Duke of Cornwall's Light Infantry (32 and 46) amalgamated to form The Somerset and Cornwall Light Infantry. On 10 July 1968 The Somerset and Cornwall Light Infantry, The King's Own Yorkshire Light Infantry (51 and 105), The King's Shropshire Light Infantry (53

and 85), and The Durham Light Infantry (68 and 106) amalgamated to form The Light Infantry.

2 *The Royal Green Jackets* (43 and 52, King's Royal Rifle Corps, Rifle Brigade) (three battalions)

On 7 November 1958 The Oxfordshire and Buckinghamshire Light Infantry (43rd and 52nd) was redesignated 1st Green Jackets (43rd and 52nd). The King's Royal Rifle Corps became 2nd Green Jackets (The King's Royal Rifle Corps), and The Rifle Brigade (Prince Consort's Own) was renamed 3rd Green Jackets (The Rifle Brigade). On 1 January 1966 all three Regiments were amalgamated as The Royal Green Jackets.

The Light Division TAVR

1 *5th Battalion The Light Infantry (Volunteers)*
2 *6th Battalion The Light Infantry (Volunteers)*
3 *7th Battalion The Light Infantry (Volunteers)*
4 *4th (Volunteer) Battalion The Royal Green Jackets*

The Parachute Regiment (one Regular battalion, one Volunteer battalion)

The Brigade of Gurkhas

1 *2nd King Edward VII's Own Gurkha Rifles (The Sirmoor Rifles)*
2 *6th Queen Elizabeth's Own Gurkha Rifles*
3 *7th Duke of Edinburgh's Own Gurkha Rifles*
4 *10th Princess Mary's Own Gurkha Rifles*
5 *The Queen's Gurkha Engineers*
6 *Queen's Gurkha Signals*
7 *Gurkha Transport Regiment*

Special Air Service Regiment (one Regular regiment and two TAVR regiments).

Army Air Corps

The remaining corps and regiments are listed below in the order of precedence.

Precedence of Regiments and Corps

The senior regiments are those of the Household Cavalry, The Life Guards followed by The Blues and Royals. Next comes the Royal Horse Artillery; but when on parade with its guns the RHA takes the right of the line and marches at the head of the Household Cavalry. The Royal Armoured Corps follows, with its regiments in the order given above — the regiments of dragoon guards first, and hussars and lancers after them, with the Royal Tank Regiment last. The order of precedence is that of the numbers of the senior of each amalgamated regiment. (The 16th/5th Lancers are an exception because the 5th Lancers were disbanded in 1799 on account of a mutinous plot and not revived till 1853; thus losing their seniority.) The Royal Artillery, Royal Engineers, and Royal Signals come next, in that order; the last Corps gets its seniority from having been formed from the Royal Engineers. Then follow the regiments of Foot Guards in the order given above. After these are the infantry regiments of the Line, taking their order from the numbers by which they were known before the amalgamations and territorial designations of 1881, and which are shown above following each title. Thus, The Royal Scots, as the 1st Foot, lead, and are followed by The Queen's Regiment which includes both the 2nd and 3rd Foot, and then The King's Own Royal Border Regiment whose senior partner is the old 4th King's Own; and so on. The Royal Green Jackets are an exception, however, because they inherit the tradition of The Rifle Brigade of being on the left of the line. They are preceded by The Parachute Regiment and the Brigade of Gurkhas, in that order. Following the Royal Green Jackets come The Special Air Service Regiment, the Army Air Corps, the Royal Army Chaplains Department, the Royal Corps of Transport, the Royal Army Medical Corps, the Royal Army Ordnance Corps, the Corps of Royal Electrical and Mechanical Engineers, the Corps of Royal Military Police, the Royal Army Pay Corps, the Royal Army Veterinary Corps, the Royal Military Academy Band Corps, the Small Arms School Corps, the Military Provost Staff Corps, the Royal Army Educational Corps, the Royal Army Dental Corps, the Royal Pioneer Corps, the Intelligence Corps, the Army Physical Training Corps, the Army Catering Corps, the General Service Corps, Queen Alexandra's Royal Nursing Corps, the Women's Royal Army Corps (but personnel on the establishment of mixed units when parading with the male element of the unit take the precedence of the unit and immediately after the men), the Royal Monmouthshire Royal Engineers (Militia) TAVR, The Honourable Artillery Company (TAVR), the remainder of the TAVR in the same order of precedence as the Regular Army, the Ulster Defence Regiment.

Index